RASPBERRY PI 5 MASTERY FOR BEGINNERS AND PROS

A Comprehensive Guide to Building Smart Home Devices Custom Electronics and Innovative Projects

TABLE OF CONTENT

CHAPTER 1

GETTING STARTED WITH RASPBERRY PI 5

In late September 2023, the Raspberry Pi Foundation announced that they would be launching the Raspberry Pi 5, the latest single-board computer. The 4GB version is priced at $60, while the 8GB version is $80. Excited about the launch, I ordered one right away, and it arrived in early November.

Having spent years amassing a colossal library of content for the Raspberry Pi 4, I look forward to doing the same with this new model. While a few operating systems are still in the works, in the coming weeks and months, they will become available. As things unfold, particularly with retro gaming, I will be reporting updates on the channel.

In the next few pages, we'll have a glance at the Raspberry Pi 5's present features and what you can presently accomplish with it!

Get your Raspberry Pi up and running fast and effectively, transforming it from a bare board to a complete computer in under 30 minutes. Begin by downloading the newest Raspberry Pi OS and flashing it onto your microSD card using the official Raspberry Pi Imager. The program formats and confirms the installation automatically for you.

Before powering it on, hook up required peripherals like a keyboard, mouse, and monitor. Plug in a stable 5V/3A power source, preferably the official USB-C charger, for optimal performance. During the first boot, run through the setup wizard to configure your Wi-Fi, location, and user credentials.

For better security, change the default password immediately, enable SSH with key-based authentication, and upgrade your system using `sudo apt update && sudo apt upgrade`. With these out of the way, your Raspberry Pi is ready to serve as a home media center, a retro game console, or an IoT hub—depending on your needs.

ESSENTIAL HARDWARE REQUIREMENTS

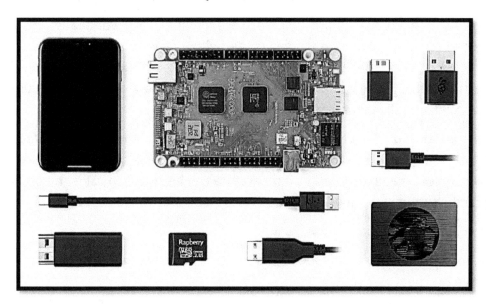

A top-down view showcasing all the essential Raspberry Pi 5 components, including the board, power adapter, microSD card, protective case, and cooling fan.

Power Supply Basics

To function reliably and smoothly, Raspberry Pi requires a reliable power supply. The power supply for newer versions is a 5V adapter with a minimum of 3A output. The official power supply for Raspberry Pi is assured to be compatible and free from issues like voltage drops, system crashes, and abrupt shutdowns. In the case of using a third-party adapter, ensure that it delivers stable power and comes with a good-quality USB-C cable.

Insufficient power can lead to problems like system instability, SD card corruption, and reduced performance. One of the signs of insufficient power supply is the display of a lightning bolt icon at the top right of the screen. To avoid these issues, do not use low-quality power supplies or cables more than 1 meter long. For usage where 24/7 operation is required or where data security is an issue, use a UPS (Uninterruptible Power Supply).

STORAGE AND COOLING ISSUES

The Raspberry Pi 5 is warmer than the earlier models, and so proper storage and cooling are required. As a storage necessity, a Class 10 or UHS-I microSD card of at least 32GB is the absolute minimum. That being said, for faster boots and improved general system performance, having an NVMe SSD on the PCIe bus is the preferred option.

Cooling is also needed, particularly when you are running heavy workloads. The official active cooler is highly recommended and comes with an easy-to-attach feature to the board. In case you need passive cooling, third-party heatsinks can be employed, but they may not suffice when you run heavy workloads. Optimal performance results from a heatsink and a small fan for a great cooling solution.

When you install your Pi, ensure there is good airflow around the case. If you are using a custom case, make sure it has airflow channels, and you may also want to drill ventilation holes if needed. Your Pi's temperature can be accessed using the on-board sensor by the terminal command:

`vcgencmd measure_temp`

Keeping the temperature at safe levels ensures that you have performance and do not suffer from overheating issues.

SETTING UP THE OPERATING SYSTEM

Preparing the microSD Card

Before installing an operating system on your Raspberry Pi, you'll need to prepare the microSD card. Insert the card into your computer using a card reader. If reusing an old card, it's best to format it first to ensure a clean installation.

Download and install the Raspberry Pi Imager from the Raspberry Pi website—there are Windows, macOS, and Linux versions. This software makes OS installation on your microSD card easy.

Open the Raspberry Pi Imager and click 'Choose OS' to select the operating system of your choice. Raspberry Pi OS (formerly Raspbian) is recommended to start with. Then, click 'Choose Storage' and select your microSD card from the available list. Double-check so as not to overwrite other drives unintentionally.

Before writing the OS image, click on the settings icon (gear icon) to configure optional settings such as hostname, SSH access, and Wi-Fi credentials. Once configured, click

'Write' and allow the process to run through. Once done, safely eject the microSD card from your computer, and your Pi is ready to be configured.

Installing Raspberry Pi OS

Starting up with your Raspberry Pi begins with installing Raspberry Pi OS. To continue, first obtain the official Raspberry Pi Imager tool on your computer by downloading and installing it. Second, insert your microSD card in your computer through a card reader.

Launch the Imager and click "Choose OS" to select the latest version of Raspberry Pi OS. If you're new to Raspberry Pi, the 64-bit version with a desktop environment is recommended. Next, click "Choose Storage" and select your microSD card from the list of available drives.

Prior to proceeding, click on the gear icon to see the advanced options. You can pre-configure settings such as hostname, WiFi credentials, and SSH access for future convenience here. You will also be able to set a username, password, keyboard layout, and time zone.

After your settings are ready, press "Write" to initiate the installation. The installation takes about 5–10 minutes, depending on the speed of your microSD card and OS version. After completion, eject the card securely and insert it into your Raspberry Pi when it is turned off.

Now plug in your monitor, keyboard, and mouse, and turn on your Raspberry Pi. Your first boot should take a few minutes while your OS sets itself up. If you've set your settings previously, you'll boot straight onto your desktop; otherwise, get through the setup wizard on the screen, which will ask you to enter in your location, password, and network details.

When you reach the desktop, open terminal and enter:

```bash```

sudo apt update && sudo apt upgrade

```

This will keep your system up to date with the latest updates and security patches.

## Preparing Your Raspberry Pi

### Network Connection

A stable internet connection is crucial for downloading updates, installing software, and setting up remote access. You can activate WiFi through either the desktop interface or the terminal.

To connect with WiFi, click the network icon in the top right, select your network, and enter your password when asked. If you are running a headless setup and need to configure WiFi, you can edit the `wpa_supplicant.conf` file in the boot partition by hand.

For a wired, simply plug in an Ethernet cable, and your Pi will be set to an IP address automatically. If you want a static one, you can go to network settings and enter in your chosen IP address, subnet mask, and gateway.

## To check your connection, open up the terminal and type in:

```bash

ping google.com

```

If you receive responses, your network is good.

For remote connection, enable SSH using the `raspi-config` tool or by creating an empty file called `ssh` within the boot partition. If your Pi will be connected to the internet, it is highly recommended that you change default passwords and maybe install a firewall for extra security.

Setting Up User Accounts

To secure your Raspberry Pi, the default username (`pi`) and password (`raspberry`) should be replaced as soon as possible. Open the terminal and enter:

```bash
passwd
```

Then follow the prompts to create a good password with a mix of letters, numbers, and special characters.

To create another user account, enter:

```bash
sudo adduser username
```

Replace `username` with your chosen name. You'll be prompted to set a password and enter optional user details. To give the new user administrative privileges, use:

```bash
sudo usermod -aG sudo username
```

For security reasons, consider disabling the default `pi` user after setting up your new account. First, test that your new user has the necessary permissions, then disable the `pi` account using:

```bash
sudo passwd -l pi
```

If you need to control a number of different users, such as in educational or business situations, you may create user groups with:

```bash
sudo groupadd groupname
```

Subsequent users are placed into the group with:

```bash
sudo usermod -aG groupname username
```

Make sure to always log out and try out new accounts before closing your configuration, so that things are functioning right.

A terminal window displaying essential configuration commands and real-time system monitoring information.

EFFICIENT MEMORY USAGE

Managing memory properly ensures your Raspberry Pi runs smoothly. To check your current memory status, open the terminal and type:

```bash
free -h
```

By default, memory is shared between the system RAM and the GPU. If you need to adjust this, you can do so in the `/boot/config.txt` file.

- For general use, 128MB of GPU memory is usually enough (`gpu_mem=128`).

- If you're using your Pi for gaming or media streaming, you might need to increase it to 256MB or more.

- Be careful—allocating too much memory to the GPU can leave your system with less RAM.

If your system runs low on memory, a swap file can act as extra virtual memory. You can create one using these commands:

```bash
sudo fallocate -l 2G /swapfile
sudo chmod 600 /swapfile
sudo mkswap /swapfile
sudo swapon /swapfile
```

To make this swap file permanent, add this line to `/etc/fstab`:

```
/swapfile swap swap defaults 0 0
```

Keep an eye on your memory usage with tools like `top` or `htop` to make sure your system is running efficiently.

Overclocking for Extra Speed

If you want a performance boost, overclocking your Raspberry Pi is an option. The Pi has built-in, safe overclocking settings that you can enable without voiding your warranty. Open the Raspberry Pi Configuration tool from the Preferences menu or run:

```bash
sudo raspi-config
```

A good starting point is the "Medium" preset, which increases the CPU speed to 1.8GHz. If your Pi runs smoothly and stays below 80°C, you can try the "High" preset for even more speed. However, overclocking generates extra heat, so a proper cooling setup—such as a heatsink or fan—is essential.

To check your Pi's temperature, use:

```bash
vcgencmd measure_temp
```

If you experience crashes or see a temperature warning, lower the overclock settings to avoid damage.

Strengthening Security

If your Raspberry Pi is connected to a network or the internet, keeping it secure is important. The first step is changing the default password for the `pi` user account:

```bash
passwd
```

For remote access, enable SSH only if necessary. If you do use SSH, enhance security by switching from password authentication to SSH keys. Generate an SSH key pair and store the public key in the `authorized_keys` file on your Pi.

Adding a firewall can help control network traffic. Install UFW (Uncomplicated Firewall) with:

```bash
sudo apt install ufw
```

Then, configure it to allow only the connections you need.

Keeping your system updated also improves security. Regularly run:

```bash
sudo apt update
sudo apt upgrade
```

To reduce the risk of unauthorized access, consider changing the default SSH port from 22 to a less common number. Installing `fail2ban` can also help by blocking repeated failed login attempts.

If your Pi is accessible online, disable any services you don't need, remove unnecessary software, and use a strong WiFi password. Hiding your WiFi network (SSID) adds another layer of security.

Finally, make regular backups using tools like `dd` or `rpi-clone` so you can quickly restore your setup if something goes wrong.

Wrapping Up

Your Raspberry Pi is now set up, optimized, and secure—ready for anything from personal projects to advanced applications.

To keep your system running smoothly, update it regularly, use strong passwords, and make backups. Whether you're interested in home automation, media centers, retro gaming, or programming, your Pi is a powerful tool with endless possibilities.

If you're new to Raspberry Pi, start with small projects and gradually explore more complex ones. Advanced users can experiment with custom configurations and even cluster multiple Pis together. No matter your experience level, the Raspberry Pi community is always there with helpful resources and ideas!

WHAT MAKES RASPBERRY PI 5 DIFFERENT

We can't wait to unveil the Raspberry Pi 5, releasing later this month at the end of October! Priced at $60 for the 4GB model and $80 for the 8GB model (plus taxes), the latest offering boasts substantial improvements across the board with an easy but very powerful user experience.

Raspberry Pi 5 is more than twice as speedy as the earlier model and marks a milestone with the first time a Raspberry Pi computer has incorporated in-house-designed silicon from Cambridge, UK.

MOST IMPORTANT FEATURES:

- Crunching Power: 2.4GHz quad-core 64-bit Arm Cortex-A76 CPU

- Enhanced Graphics: VideoCore VII GPU with OpenGL ES 3.1 and Vulkan 1.2 support

- Dual 4K Display Support: Two HDMI outputs at 4K 60fps

- Improved Connectivity: Dual-band Wi-Fi (802.11ac), Bluetooth 5.0, and Gigabit Ethernet with PoE+ support

- Faster Storage: High-speed microSD card interface with SDR104 mode

- Additional Ports: 2x USB 3.0 (5Gbps), 2x USB 2.0, and PCIe 2.0 x1 for high-speed peripherals

- Camera & Display Improvements: Two 4-lane MIPI transceivers

- Convenience Features: Real-time clock, standard 40-pin GPIO header, and power button

We're releasing the Raspberry Pi 5 ahead of its arrival in shops for the first time in years. Pre-orders are currently available from our Approved Resellers, with deliveries starting at the end of October.

We're just very thankful to the passionate makers and techies community that have helped make Raspberry Pi what we are today. The past few years have not been easy with supply chain bottlenecks, and we're truly thankful to your patience. As a token of our gratitude, we're prioritizing individual buyers by reserving all Raspberry Pi 5 units for single-unit sales until at least the end of the year—ensuring our community gets first access. Also, readers of The MagPi and HackSpace magazines will get a one-time code as a subscriber, which will allow them to access Raspberry Pi 5 hardware early. If you want early access, look at our Priority Boarding program. New subscribers can also benefit from this offer!

LOOKING BACK AT THE JOURNEY

Since its launch in June 2019, the Raspberry Pi 4 has been a game-changer, bringing PC-class performance to the Raspberry Pi family. Equipped with a 1.5GHz quad-core Arm Cortex-A72 processor, it was 40 times faster than the initial 2012 release. Its arrival could not have been timed better—when schools shut down in early 2020, thousands of students made the Raspberry Pi 4 their primary computer for homeschooling.

Over the last four years, Raspberry Pi 4, and the Raspberry Pi 400 and Compute Module 4, have become increasingly popular with hobbyists, educators, and engineers. As a result of firmware enhancements, newer Raspberry Pi 4 boards now run at 1.8GHz, 20% faster than the original launch model. Despite supply chain challenges, over 14 million units of Raspberry Pi 4 have been manufactured and dispatched during this time.

THE FUTURE GENERATION: RASPBERRY PI 5

The demand for better performance is only growing, and we've been prepping towards this for six years now, since 2016 in the Raspberry Pi 3 era. The fruit of all that effort over the years is finally here: the Raspberry Pi 5—with 2 to 3 times higher CPU and GPU performance than the Pi 4, double the memory and I/O bandwidth, and, for the first time ever, Raspberry Pi's own custom silicon driving a flagship product.

A Brand-New Platform with Custom Chips

Raspberry Pi 5 has three custom chips, specifically designed for this new model. These chips work together to deliver a significant performance boost, keeping Raspberry Pi at the forefront.

An Entirely New Platform with a Powerful Chipset

Raspberry Pi 5 introduces an entirely new platform, powered by three custom chips designed specifically for this device. These new components, working in unison, bring a staggering performance boost, pushing the speed and efficiency benchmark.

The core of this upgrade is the BCM2712 processor, designed to increase computing power and handle more laborious tasks without perspiring.

Better Performance with a New Chipset

The BCM2712 is Broadcom's cutting-edge 16-nanometer processor, designed to replace the 28-nanometer BCM2711 that powered the Raspberry Pi 4. It has remarkable architectural upgrades, including a quad-core 64-bit Arm Cortex-A76 CPU running at 2.4GHz, with 512KB L2 cache per core and a 2MB shared L3 cache. This new architecture is three generations ahead of the Cortex-A72 that drives the Pi 4 and offers greater efficiency per instruction and performance per clock. With its faster core, increased clock speed, and more efficient process, the Raspberry Pi 5 offers a substantial speed boost at reduced power usage. Accompanying the improved CPU is the VideoCore VII GPU, a Cambridge-designed one supported by fully open-source Mesa drivers courtesy of Igalia.

The GPU provides dual 4Kp60 HDMI output, much better than the Pi 4's single 4Kp60 or dual 4Kp30 support. It has a 4Kp60 HEVC decoder as well, along with an improved Image Sensor Pipeline (ISP) by Raspberry Pi that enhances multimedia performance. To enable these enhancements, the LPDDR4X SDRAM is being run at 4267MT/s, raising the effective memory bandwidth of the Raspberry Pi 4 by more than two times.

RP1: A New Way of I/O

On previous Raspberry Pi boards, most input/output (I/O) operations were integrated into the main processor.

Some operations were being handled by external components, such as the VL805 USB controller for the Pi 4 or Microchip LAN controllers in earlier models. But with the passage of time and the advancement of technology, and processors moving towards more efficient production processes, relying on a monolithic design alone is technically cumbersome and costly. Therefore, the manufacturers decided to implement a more efficient way of I/O management for the Raspberry Pi 5.

A NEW ARCHITECTURE FOR RASPBERRY PI 5

In contrast to the earlier models, the Raspberry Pi 5 employs a disaggregated chiplet architecture. Only the high-speed digital functions such as SDRAM, HDMI, PCI Express, and the SD card interface (because of layout considerations) remain directly connected to the main processor (BCM2712). All other I/O functions are controlled by an auxiliary controller, RP1, which is realized in a more cost-effective process and linked to the main processor via PCI Express.

Introducing RP1: The I/O Controller Single-Minded Dedication to the Task

The RP1 I/O controller was designed by the same Raspberry Pi team that developed the RP2040 microcontroller. As with the RP2040, it's based on TSMC's 40LP process, a low-cost, mature technology. The controller handles the task of managing:

- Two USB 3.0 and two USB 2.0 ports
- Gigabit Ethernet connectivity
- Two four-lane MIPI transceivers for cameras and displays
- Analog video output
- 3.3V general-purpose I/O (GPIO)
- Various low-speed interfaces (UART, SPI, I2C, I2S, and PWM)

RP1 is connected to the BCM2712 via a four-lane PCI Express 2.0 interface for a fast 16Gb/s data connection.

It is a project that has been under development since 2016, constituting the longest, most intricate, and costliest endeavor in the history of Raspberry Pi, with an overall investment of $15 million. The Raspberry Pi 5's utilized C0 revision is the third significant revision of the RP1, tweaked to provide high compatibility with Raspberry Pi models before it.

DA9091: Optimized Power Management

To support BCM2712 and RP1, Raspberry Pi 5 also includes the Renesas DA9091 "Gilmour" power management IC (PMIC). The advanced power controller has eight independent power supplies, a quad-phase core supply capable of delivering 20 amps of current—delivering stable and efficient power to the Cortex-A76 cores and other digital circuitry in BCM2712.

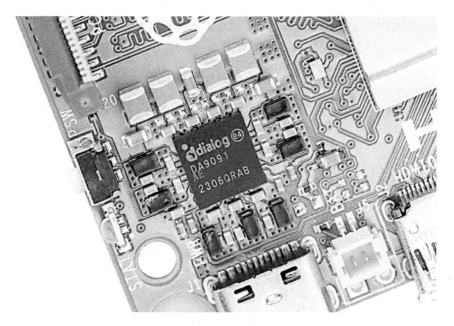

A TAILORED POWER MANAGEMENT SOLUTION

Like BCM2712, the DA9091 power management IC (PMIC) too is the result of a multi-year partnership. Raspberry Pi engineers worked in close cooperation with Renesas' Edinburgh team and designed a power management chip tailored to their needs. This also gave the chance for two features highly desired:

✔ **A real-time clock (RTC)** – Driven by an external supercapacitor or a rechargeable lithium-manganese cell when the board is off for keeping time.

✔ **A PC-style power button** – Both soft and hard power-off/on function for easier power state control.

RETAINED FEATURES FROM RASPBERRY PI 4

While much of the chipset is new, two of the most critical pieces from the Raspberry Pi 4 are carried over with some enhancements:

✔ **Wi-Fi & Bluetooth:** The Infineon CYW43455 combo chip still offers dual-band 802.11ac Wi-Fi and Bluetooth 5.0 (with BLE), but with a dedicated switched power supply for improved energy efficiency. It also uses an enhanced SDIO interface with DDR50 mode support for higher data throughput.

✔ **Ethernet:** The Broadcom BCM54213 Gigabit Ethernet PHY continues to handle wired networking. However, it now sits at a 45-degree angle, an unusual design choice that may disappoint those who prefer a more traditional, aligned layout—including Raspberry Pi's CTO of Software, Gordon Hollingworth.

Refinements to the Raspberry Pi 5 Form Factor

At first glance, the Raspberry Pi 5 looks very similar to its predecessors, still with its compact, credit-card-sized shape. However, some modifications have been made to leverage the features of the new chipset:

✔️ **Removal of the Composite Video/Audio Jack**: The previous four-pole audio and composite video jack has been removed. However, composite video output is still available via two 0.1\ "-spaced pads at the bottom of the board.

✔️ **New FPC Camera & Display Connectors:** The board features two four-lane MIPI interfaces as replacements for the earlier camera connector and four-pole jack. These use a higher-density pinout, the same one found on Compute Module I/O boards. Both connectors are bi-directional, i.e., they can be used for either a CSI-2 camera or a DSI display.

✔️ **Dedicated PCI Express Connector**: A smaller FPC connector is provided on the left side of the board (where the old display connector used to be). This provides a single-lane PCI Express 2.0 interface, enabling high-speed peripheral expansion.

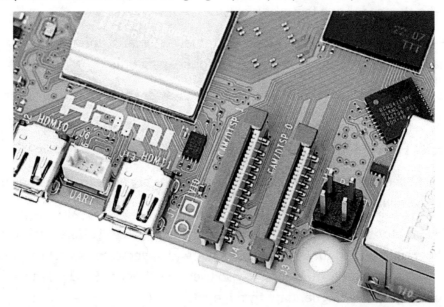

The Gigabit Ethernet port is back in its usual place at the bottom right of the board from its brief sojourn at the top right on the Raspberry Pi 4. Accompanying it is the four-pin

PoE connector, which cleans up the board design but renders the board incompatible with older PoE and PoE+ HATs.

Additionally, the board now features mounting holes for a heatsink, and JST connectors for the following functions: a two-pin connector for the RTC battery, a three-pin connector for Arm debug and UART, and a four-pin connector for a fan with PWM control and tacho feedback.

Designed in Cambridge, Made in Wales

Like other flagship Raspberry Pi models, the Raspberry Pi 5 is manufactured at Sony UK Technology Centre in Pencoed, South Wales. Since partnering with Sony for the launch of the original Raspberry Pi in 2012, the proximity has allowed for more integrated design and mass production. Having manufacturing just a few hours from our Cambridge engineering design centre has allowed us to create products that are dependable, low-cost, and easy to produce in volume.

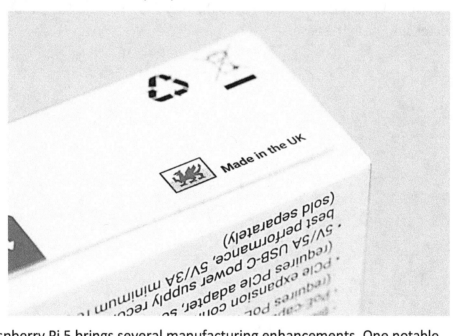

The Raspberry Pi 5 brings several manufacturing enhancements. One notable enhancement is the use of intrusive reflow for connectors, which makes it more robust, enhances production efficiency, and does away with the need for energy-consuming selective or wave soldering. Other enhancements include full routing panel singulation for smoother board edges and a new production test regime derived from the large-scale testing of the RP2040 microcontroller.

New and Improved Accessories

Every new flagship Raspberry Pi model is launched alongside updated accessories, and the Raspberry Pi 5 is no different. Layout changes, new interfaces, and improved peak performance—at the expense of a modest rise in power consumption—have necessitated both redesigns of old favourites and some brand-new accessories.

Redesigned Case

The $10 Raspberry Pi 5 case keeps the same form factor as the Raspberry Pi 4 case but includes several improvements for better usability and thermal management.

It has an integrated fan, capable of moving up to 2.79 CFM, with fluid dynamic bearings for quieter, longer life. It connects to the four-pin JST socket on the Raspberry Pi 5 to provide temperature-controlled cooling. Air is drawn in through a 360-degree slot beneath the lid, across a heatsink mounted to the BCM2712 AP, and out through vents and connector cutouts in the base.

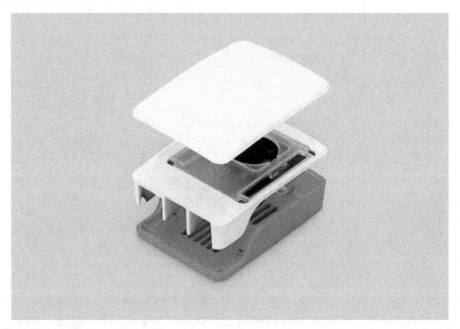

Raspberry Pi 5 case has been slightly extended, with the features for retention changed so that the board can be put in without having to remove the SD card. The top of the case is also removable, allowing for stacking several cases or mounting HATs on top of the fan using spacers and GPIO header extensions.

Like all of our plastic products, this new case is manufactured by T-Zero in the West Midlands, UK.

Active Cooling Option

The Raspberry Pi 5 is designed to run with standard workloads without a case or active cooling. For those needing the board to be continuously running heavy loads without throttling, a new Active Cooler can be ordered as an option for $5. The cooler attaches to the board via two new mounting holes and connects to the same four-pin JST port as the case fan.

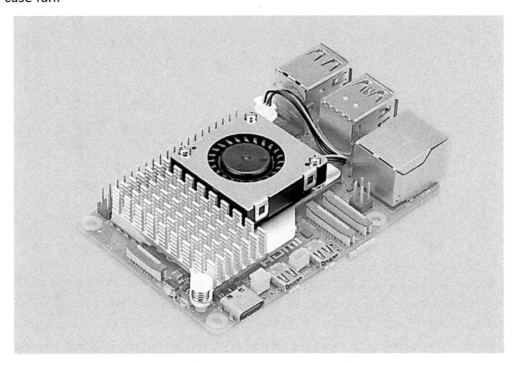

The Raspberry Pi 5 Active Cooler is designed with low noise and long-life performance. It utilizes a radial blower to blow air through a precisely machined aluminum heatsink, which efficiently dissipates heat. Together, the case and Active Cooler maintain the Raspberry Pi 5's temperature well within acceptable limits, even under heavy loads and standard room temperatures. However, the Active Cooler offers even better cooling performance, and so it's a great option for those who like to overclock the system.

27W USB-C Power Supply

The Raspberry Pi 5 is power-greedy compared to the earlier version, the Raspberry Pi 4, when handling the same workload. However, as it offers much higher performance, it can consume up to 12W of power while handling heavy tasks, compared to 8W on the Raspberry Pi 4.

Using a standard 5V, 3A (15W) USB-C power supply, the system will automatically limit the supplied USB power output to 600mA to offer a stable operation under heavy loads. This is less than the 1.2A limit on the Raspberry Pi 4, but that is sufficient for standard accessories like keyboards, mice, and other low-power peripherals.

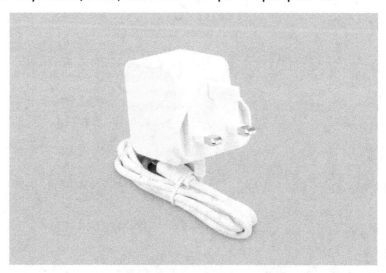

If you need to power hungry peripherals like SSDs or external hard drives and still have some headroom for peak workloads, we offer a $12 USB-C power adapter. The adapter is rated at 5V, 5A (25W), and when detected by the Raspberry Pi 5 firmware, it raises the USB current limit to 1.6A. This provides an extra 5W for connected USB devices and an extra 5W for the board, ideal for those users looking to dabble in overclocking. If you're using a 3A adapter, you can manually override the present limit to achieve the same outcomes. Our tests show that in this mode, the Raspberry Pi 5 works fine with most high-power USB setups, except for the most excessive loads.

CAMERA AND DISPLAY CABLES

The Raspberry Pi 5 features new higher-density MIPI connectors, so you'll need an adapter to connect cameras, displays, or third-party accessories.

To offer compatibility with existing Raspberry Pi cameras and displays, we have FPC adapter cables that convert the new "mini" format to the older "standard" format. The cables come in 200mm ($1), 300mm ($2), and 500mm ($3) lengths, providing flexible options for different setups.

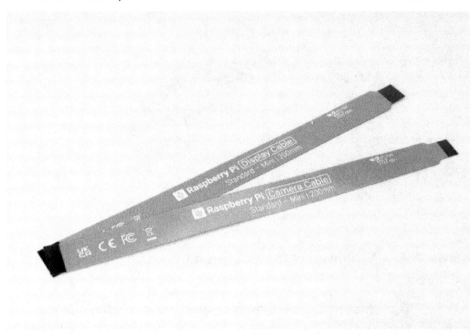

The Camera Module 3, High-Quality Camera, Global Shutter Camera, and Touchscreen Display will all be provided with two types of cable: a standard-to-standard cable and a 200mm mini-to-standard cable, so that they are usable across the range of configurations.

PoE+ HAT

From early 2024, a new PoE+ HAT will be available. The new version is designed for the repositioned four-pin PoE header of the Raspberry Pi 5. It has an L-shaped form factor, so it can be seated comfortably in the Raspberry Pi 5 case without obstructing airflow or other components.

A hand-soldered prototype of this L-shaped PoE+ HAT has been built for testing with the Raspberry Pi 5.

The prototype PoE+ HAT here is not the final version, and the final production model will look different.

The new PoE+ HAT is efficient and performance-oriented, and it has a planar transformer built into the PCB design. It also utilizes an optimized flyback converter design, offering high efficiency throughout the range of power outputs from 0 to 25W.

M.2 HATs and PCI Express Expansion

One of the most thrilling upgrades in the Raspberry Pi 5 is the single-lane PCI Express 2.0 interface, intended for high-speed peripherals. This interface is available through a 16-pin, 0.5mm pitch FPC connector on the left-hand side of the board.

Beginning in early 2024, Raspberry Pi will release two mechanical adapter boards to link this interface to M.2 NVMe SSDs and other M.2 accessories:

✔. Standard HAT Form Factor Adapter –. For larger devices, allowing users to mount and utilize full-sized peripherals.

✔ L-Shaped Adapter – Similar to the PoE+ HAT's L-shaped form factor and used for 2230- and 2242-format SSDs, allowing them to be mounted within the Raspberry Pi 5 case for a neat and unobtrusive setup.

Prototype M.2 HAT. Final hardware will not look like this.

Raspberry Pi Beginner's Guide, 5th Edition

The latest edition of the Raspberry Pi Beginner's Guide boasts a new layout and is available for £19.99 ($24.99). As the definitive guide for Raspberry Pi users, this edition has been fully revised to cover Raspberry Pi 5 and the upcoming Raspberry Pi OS based on Debian Bookworm.

Real-Time Clock (RTC) Battery

To supply the real-time clock (RTC) of Raspberry Pi 5 when there is no power source, a Panasonic lithium manganese rechargeable coin cell has been purchased. The battery is pre-installed with a two-pin JST plug and an adhesive mounting pad for easy installation. It is priced at $5 and gives confidence that the RTC keeps correct time even when there is no main power.

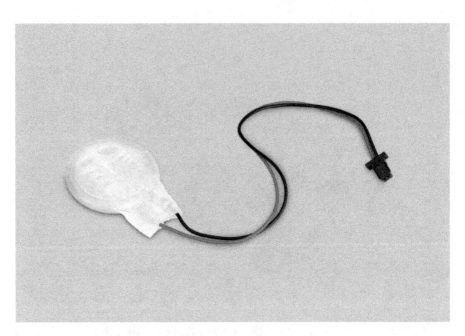

A New and Improved Raspberry Pi OS

With Raspberry Pi 5 released, the software team has been working hard on developing an improved version of Raspberry Pi OS, the default operating system of Raspberry Pi. The new version is based on Debian "Bookworm" and brings a plethora of improvements, such as the switch from X11 to the Wayfire Wayland compositor on Raspberry Pi 4 and 5, along with an enhanced and more modern user interface.

The new Raspberry Pi OS will be available in mid-October and will be the officially supported operating system for Raspberry Pi 5. Watch this space for more details, and be ready to download it just before Raspberry Pi 5 hits the shelves in late October.

Acknowledgments

The development of Raspberry Pi 5 has been a seven-year journey, with a $25 million investment and work done by dozens of organizations and hundreds of individuals. A full list of the individuals involved in bringing Raspberry Pi 5 into existence—though the full list for those involved in its custom silicon development—is available for those interested to learn more.

RASPBERRY PI 4 VS. RASPBERRY PI 5: WHAT'S NEW?

Whether you are deciding between the Raspberry Pi 4 and the newest Raspberry Pi 5, both are excellent choices among single-board computers (SBCs).

But the Raspberry Pi 5 is no minor upgrade—it raises the bar with a faster processor, improved graphics, and increased connectivity options. This new one offers more power, performance, and versatility, a huge leap forward.

But how significant is the difference really? Is it an upgrade worth it? Let's break it down.

Hardware Comparison: Raspberry Pi 4 vs. Raspberry Pi 5

Here is how the two models compare in regards to significant hardware specifications:

Hardware Specs	Raspberry Pi 4	Raspberry Pi 5
Processor	Quad-core Cortex-A72, 1.5 GHz	Quad-core Cortex-A76, 2.4 GHz
RAM Options	1GB, 2GB, 4GB, 8GB LPDDR4	2GB, 4GB, 8GB LPDDR4X
Graphics (GPU)	VideoCore VI, 500 MHz, OpenGL ES 3.1, Vulkan 1.0	VideoCore VII, 800 MHz, OpenGL ES 3.1, Vulkan 1.2
Storage	MicroSD, USB 3.0 boot support	MicroSD, PCIe Gen 2 slot, USB 3.0 boot support
USB Ports	2 × USB 2.0, 2 × USB 3.0	2 × USB 2.0, 2 × USB 3.0
Networking	Gigabit Ethernet, Wi-Fi 802.11ac, Bluetooth 5.0	Gigabit Ethernet, Wi-Fi 802.11ac, Bluetooth 5.0
GPIO Pins	40-pin GPIO	40-pin GPIO
Power Supply	5V/3A USB-C	5V/5A USB-C
Display Support	2 × Micro HDMI, up to 4K (single display)	2 × Micro HDMI, up to 4K (dual display) with HDR support
Additional Features	PoE HAT support, MIPI DSI, MIPI CSI	PoE+ HAT support, PCIe 2.0, MIPI DSI, MIPI CSI

Raspberry Pi 5's Key Improvements

First, the Raspberry Pi 5 can appear nearly identical to its predecessor, but it features several major upgrades:

✔ **Faster Processor** – Upgraded to a Cortex-A76 (2.4 GHz), which provides significantly better processing power.

✔ **Enhanced Graphics** – The new VideoCore VII GPU runs at 800 MHz, with Vulkan 1.2 support for enhanced rendering and performance.

✔ **Enhanced Storage Options** – PCIe Gen 2 support allows faster storage with NVMe SSDs, ideal for high-speed applications.

✔ **Enhanced Display & Multimedia** – Supports dual 4K displays with HDR support for better colors and video quality.

✔ **Increased Power Capacity** – A 5V/5A USB-C power supply delivers more stable power supply to power-hungry peripherals.

✔ **PCIe Expansion** – A second PCIe 2.0 slot offers faster external storage and add-on accessories.

The Raspberry Pi 5 is a substantial upgrade over the Pi 4, especially for those who need higher performance, better graphics, and enhanced expandability. Whether you're into DIY projects, media centers, robotics, or even AI applications, this new version offers more flexibility and power than ever before.

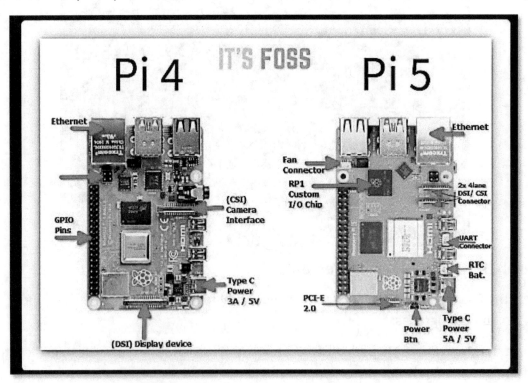

A side-by-side hardware comparison between Pi 4 and Pi 5

WHAT IS NEW IN RASPBERRY PI 5?

The biggest upgrade in Raspberry Pi 5 is the inclusion of a PCIe Gen 2 slot, which offers faster storage and expansion using an adapter.

Another major improvement is in camera and display connectivity. The old DSI and CSI ports are substituted with two four-lane MIPI interfaces, and it becomes easier to connect peripherals like cameras and displays.

The Raspberry Pi 5 also features:

✔ A built-in power button for on/off switching ease.

✔ A real-time clock (RTC), but you will need to add a battery to enable it.

One of the most significant changes is the addition of the RP1 chip, which allocates processing power to all I/O operations. This leads to better efficiency in handling devices like USB peripherals, cameras, displays, and networking.

Power Requirements: What You Need to Know

The power requirements of the Raspberry Pi 4 and Pi 5 are quite different.

✔ The Raspberry Pi 4 operates on a 5V, 3A power supply, which is backward compatible with most chargers.

✔ The Raspberry Pi 5, however, requires a 5V, 5A power supply to meet its higher power requirements.

This means that the application of an incompatible or lower-wattage power supply may lead to undervoltage issues and unstable operation. To avoid this, it's recommended to use the official Raspberry Pi 5 power adapter for ensured performance.

Heat Management: Do You Need Cooling?

With more power comes more heat, and that's where cooling solutions are introduced.

✔ The Raspberry Pi 4 can cope with heat employing passive cooling fundamentals (e.g., heatsinks). However, when you're performing demanding tasks, active cooling (i.e., fans) is recommended.

✔ The Raspberry Pi 5, with its more powerful CPU and increased power consumption, becomes significantly warmer. During our tests, while no thermal throttling was observed, the Pi 5 became quite hot to the touch.

To prevent overheating and get the best out of performance, it is highly recommended to invest in active cooling systems such as fans or high-efficiency heatsinks.

For a great cooling case, check out Abhishek's Pironman 5 case review, which has a good cooling system for the Raspberry Pi 5.

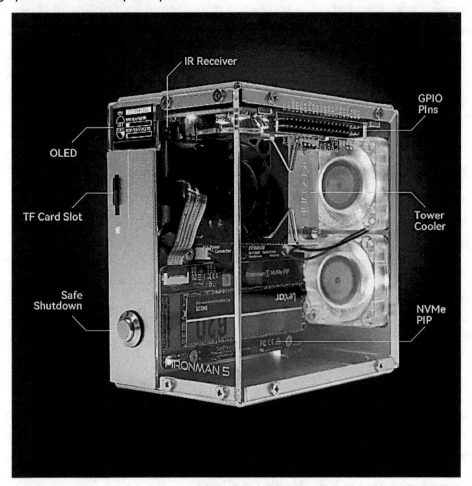

Pironman 5 Case: Expansion and Cooling in One Package

The Pironman 5 case is a cooling-focused performance package specifically designed for the Raspberry Pi 5. It comes with a tower heatsink and two RGB fans for maximum temperature control even with high-demand applications.

In addition to cooling, the case also enhances functionality, with:

✔ A M.2 SSD slot for faster storage and reliability.

✔ Two standard HDMI ports, providing more flexibility for display connections.

If you're looking to keep your Raspberry Pi 5 cool while also expanding its capabilities, the Pironman 5 case is a solid choice.

Performance Benchmark: How Raspberry Pi 4 Competes Against Pi 5

Now that the significant differences are out of the way, let's have a glance at the performance benchmarks to determine how big an improvement the Raspberry Pi 5 really is.

While it's clear that the Pi 5 has superior hardware, the question is actually: How much quicker will it be? And more importantly, do you actually need the extra power for your work?

If the Pi 4 is already working your tasks just fine, then you may not require an upgrade. But if you're looking for more efficiency and higher performance, the Pi 5 might be worth the cost.

To make an impartial comparison, I ran both models through Geekbench and Sysbench tests: Geekbench tests CPU and GPU performance, giving a good estimate of processing power. Sysbench performs multicore efficiency and memory handling tests, showing how well both boards handle heavy loads.

Let's have a look at the specifications of the Raspberry Pi models I used before getting to the numbers:

	Raspberry Pi 5 Model B Rev 1.0	Raspberry Pi 4 Model B Rev 1.5
Operating System	**Debian GNU/Linux 12 (bookworm)**	**Debian GNU/Linux 12 (bookworm)**
Model	Raspberry Pi 5 Model B Rev 1.0	Raspberry Pi 4 Model B Rev 1.5
Processor	ARM BCM2835 @ 2.40 GHz 1 Processor, 1 Core, 4 Threads	ARM BCM2835 @ 1.80 GHz 1 Processor, 1 Core, 4 Threads
Processor ID	ARM Implementer 65 architecture 8 variant 4 part 3339 revision 1	ARM Implementer 65 architecture 8 variant 0 part 3336 revision 3
L1 Instruction Cache		
L1 Data Cache		
L2 Cache		
L3 Cache		
Motherboard	N/A	N/A
BIOS		
Memory	7.86 GB	3.71 GB

Specs of the Raspberry Pi's that I used for testing

Geekbench Comparison of Performance

At the head of the class is Geekbench, which provides an excellent measure of CPU and GPU performance. Numbers don't deceive—both single-core and multi-core score highlight the apparent performance difference between the Raspberry Pi 4 and the Raspberry Pi 5.

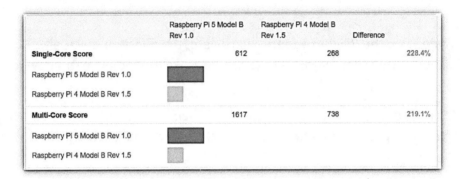

	Raspberry Pi 5 Model B Rev 1.0	Raspberry Pi 4 Model B Rev 1.5	Difference
Single-Core Score	612	268	228.4%
Raspberry Pi 5 Model B Rev 1.0			
Raspberry Pi 4 Model B Rev 1.5			
Multi-Core Score	1617	738	219.1%
Raspberry Pi 5 Model B Rev 1.0			
Raspberry Pi 4 Model B Rev 1.5			

Looking closer at the Geekbench scores, the Raspberry Pi 5 has an enormous performance boost over the Pi 4. Among these are faster text compression, improved image processing, and improved HTML5 performance, making it a more powerful and efficient device for demanding tasks.

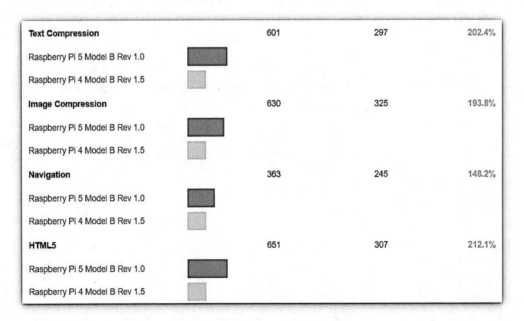

Text Compression	601	297	202.4%
Raspberry Pi 5 Model B Rev 1.0			
Raspberry Pi 4 Model B Rev 1.5			
Image Compression	630	325	193.8%
Raspberry Pi 5 Model B Rev 1.0			
Raspberry Pi 4 Model B Rev 1.5			
Navigation	363	245	148.2%
Raspberry Pi 5 Model B Rev 1.0			
Raspberry Pi 4 Model B Rev 1.5			
HTML5	651	307	212.1%
Raspberry Pi 5 Model B Rev 1.0			
Raspberry Pi 4 Model B Rev 1.5			

The Geekbench scores of both Raspberry Pi 4 and Pi 5 also indicate performance gains in significant real-world scenarios, such as text and image compression, navigation, and HTML5 tasks. These equate to quicker and smoother day-to-day operations.

Sysbench Performance

When compared with Sysbench, the Raspberry Pi 5 once more outperformed the Pi 4, demonstrating its improved CPU performance.

✔ **Event Processing Speed** – The Pi 5 executed 4,155 events per second, while on the Pi 4 it was 2,766 events per second, which indicates a substantial improvement in processing power.

✔ **Lower Latency** – The Pi 5 averaged at 0.96 ms latency, significantly lower than the 1.44 ms of the Pi 4, meaning that it will be more responsive when under load.

Through its improved architecture, the Pi 5 delivers smoother performance, faster execution, and better handling of resource-intensive tasks.

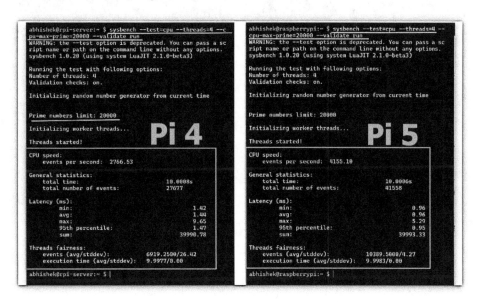

Sysbench multicore benchmark between Pi 4 & Pi 5

Memory Performance: A Clear Winner

As expected from an improved machine, the Raspberry Pi 5 offers significant improvements in memory performance compared to the Pi 4.

✔️ **Faster Memory Operations** – The Pi 5 processed 37.1 million operations per second, a notable increase over the Pi 4's 25.1 million, showing considerably improved memory handling.

✔️ **Faster Transfer Speeds** – The Pi 5 achieved a memory transfer rate of 3631 MiB/sec, surpassing the Pi 4's 2452 MiB/sec, enabling quicker data movement.

✔️ **Steady Latency** – Despite having more to process, the Pi 5 had uniform response times, with minimal to no lag in memory-intensive tasks.

With enhanced memory bandwidth and lower latency, the Pi 5 is a more effective choice for applications that require a lot of resources and rely heavily on fast data access.

Sysbench Memory speed test (RAM) between Pi 4 & Pi 5

Price Comparison: How Much Does It Cost?

The Raspberry Pi 4 and Pi 5 both have different price points, which correspond to the feature set and level of performance.

✔️ **Raspberry Pi 4** – Typically ranges from $35 to $55, based on the RAM version and where you buy it.

✔ **Raspberry Pi 5** – More expensive, usually between $60 and $80, because of its superior hardware and extra features.

While the Pi 5 is more expensive, both models offer great value for the respective needs. To get the best value, it's a good practice to check a few retailers before purchasing.

Final Thoughts: Which One Should You Choose?

While benchmarks give a good measure of performance, they don't show the whole picture.

✔ **Real-World Use** – In real-world use, the Pi 5 gives noticeable improvements, but everything isn't dramatically different.

✔ **Day-to-Day Performance** – The biggest difference? Smoother YouTube video playback and faster boot times with the Pi 5, especially with Raspberry Pi OS Desktop.

✔ **Memory plays a role** – My Pi 5 was 8GB of RAM, while my Pi 4 was 4GB, which might be responsible for some of the overall smoothness differences.

At the end of the day, the Raspberry Pi 5 is a huge step forward, thanks to:

☑ A faster CPU

☑ Better memory performance

☑ New features like a dedicated power button and the game-changing PCIe interface

If you need extra power and expanded capabilities, the Pi 5 is the way to go. But if you're on a budget, the Pi 4 still holds up well for many projects.

UNBOXING AND SETTING UP THE BOARD

When you unbox your Raspberry Pi 5 kit, you'll find the following and why each item is significant.

✔ **Official Case** – While not required, using the official case helps in protecting your Pi 5 from accidental drops or damage.

✔️ **Power Supply** – The 27W USB-C power adapter is specifically made for the Pi 5. Although a Pi 4 power supply may be compatible, this one guarantees your device receives the power it needs to run smoothly.

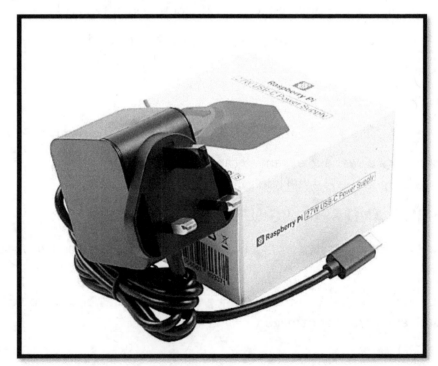

✔️ **Active Cooler** – Your Pi 5 needs to stay cool. If it gets too hot, it will slow down because of thermal throttling, so a cooling solution is strongly advised.

✔ **HDMI Cable & MakerDisk SD Card** – The HDMI cable is inserted into the micro HDMI ports, and the MakerDisk microSD card provides reliable performance. (Bonus: The OS is preinstalled on the MakerDisk!)

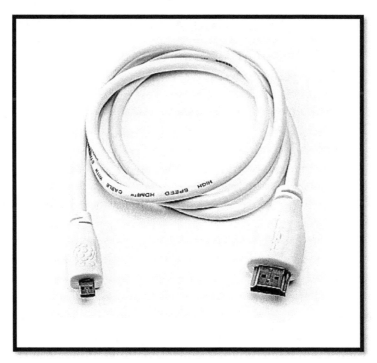

A Quick Glimpse at the Raspberry Pi 5's Hardware

✔ Processor – Powered by the Broadcom BCM2712 chipset, featuring:

- 64-bit ARM Cortex-A76 architecture (ARMv8-A ISA)

- Quad-core processor based on a 16nm SoC

- Operates at 2.4GHz with optimized performance

- 64KB L1 cache, 512KB L2 cache per core, and a 2MB shared L3 cache

- Metal body for enhanced heat dissipation

✔ Memory (SDRAM) – The Pi 5 is equipped with LPDDR4X-4267 RAM and comes in:

- 8GB

- 4GB

- 2GB

Despite all these upgrades, the Raspberry Pi 5 still retains its compact, credit card-sized form factor, making it just as portable and versatile as ever!

RASPBERRY PI 5 MAJOR FEATURES

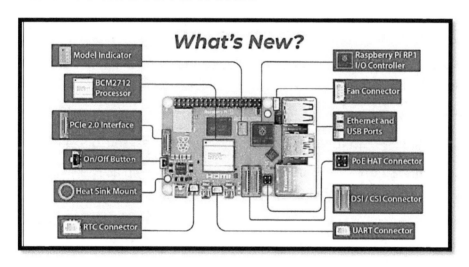

RASPBERRY PI 5: PORTS, INSTALLATION, AND OS INSTALLATION

Ports & Connectivity

Following is a description of the principal ports and connectors on the Raspberry Pi 5 and their purposes:

- **SD Card Slot** – Still located on the bottom of the board, just like previous versions.

- **Gigabit Ethernet Port –** Now on the left side, as compared to the Pi 4, where it was on the far right.

- **USB 3.0 Ports** – Two high-speed ports in the middle, offering up to 5 Gbps for fast data transfers.

- **USB 2.0 Ports** – Two standard ports on the far right, ideal for peripherals like a keyboard and mouse.

- **Fan Connector** – A dedicated connector to connect the active cooler to keep temperatures in check.

- **MIPI DSI & CSI Ports** – Two ports to connect displays and cameras.

- **Micro HDMI Ports** – Dual micro-HDMI outputs with 720p, 1080p, and 4K support.

- **USB-C Port –** To power the Raspberry Pi 5.

- **40 GPIO Pins** – Facilitates expansion with accessories, sensors, and HATs.

- **PCIe Express Port** – A 16-pin 0.5mm FFC connector replaces the DSI port, widening the single-lane PCIe Gen 2 bus. It accommodates:

  - ✓ NVMe SSDs

  - ✓ Network Cards

  - ✓ Graphics Cards

  - ✓ HATs and M.2 devices (See the official M.2 HAT+ from Raspberry Pi!)

✔ **Heat Sink Mount** – A specific place to mount a heat sink for improved cooling.

✔ **RTC Connector** – Enables attachment to a Real-Time Clock (RTC) module to keep accurate time even when the Pi is not powered on.

✔ **UART Connector** – To communicate with external devices via UART (Universal Asynchronous Receiver-Transmitter).

✔ **PoE HAT Connector** – Supports Power over Ethernet (PoE), in which the Raspberry Pi can be powered via an Ethernet cable.

✔ **On/Off Button** – A standalone power button for simple on/off—a convenience feature in this release.

HARDWARE SETUP

✔ Installing the Active Cooler

Connect the cooler to the fan port, ensuring the thermal pad is in place.

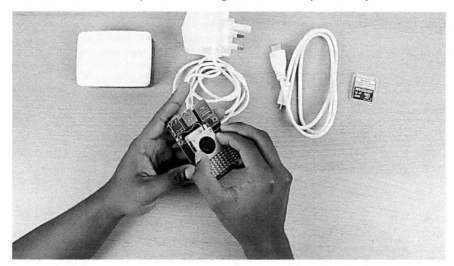

✔ **Installing the Case**

Fit the Raspberry Pi 5 into the case.

Tip: If using the active cooler, the top cover of the case will not be able to fit.

✔ Final Hardware Check

Make sure the Pi 5 is properly installed with the active cooler and case.

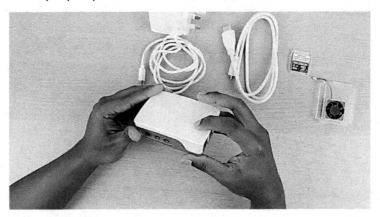

Software Setup: Installing the OS

✔ SD Card Preparation

Insert the microSD card into a card reader and then into your computer.

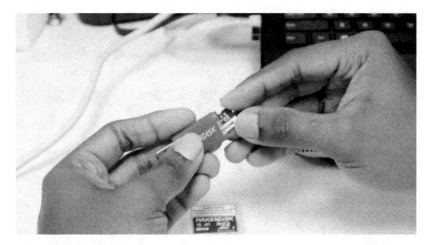

✔ Downloading & Installing Raspberry Pi Imager

Open your browser and type in "Raspberry Pi Imager."

Download the installer appropriate for your operating system (Windows, macOS, or Linux).

Install and launch the software.

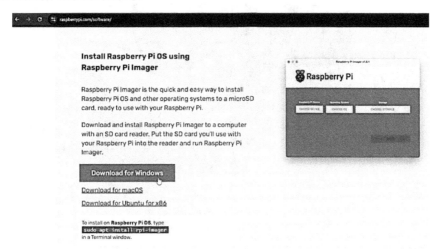

✔ Flashing the OS onto the SD Card

- Open Raspberry Pi Imager and choose your device.
- Select "Raspberry Pi OS (64-bit)" as the OS.
- Select the microSD card as the drive.

Note: Turn off any other external drives to avoid flashing the incorrect drive!

Use any custom settings if needed.

Start the flashing process, and then eject the SD card once it has finished.

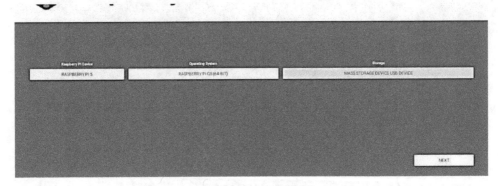

Getting Started with Raspberry Pi 5: First Boot & Setup

1. Powering Up

- Insert your microSD card into the Raspberry Pi 5.

- Connect the power supply and turn it on.

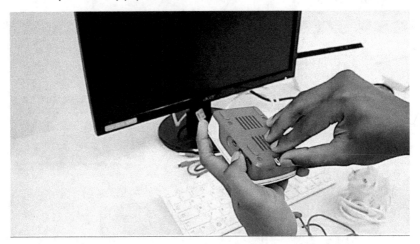

2. Initial Setup

- Select country & language settings.

- Connect to Wi-Fi. Alternatively, use the LAN cable to access the internet.

- Configure your network settings as necessary.

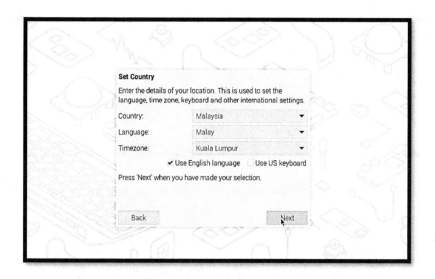

choose your country

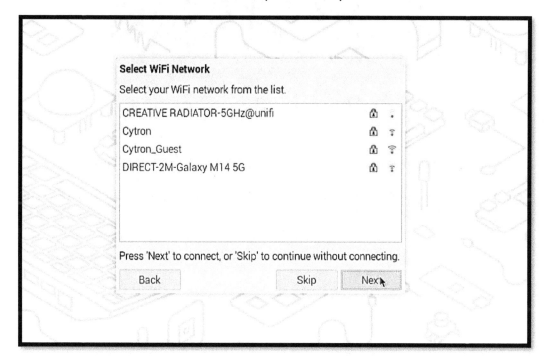

Set your Wi-Fi network

3. Updating Software

For security and functionality, it is good practice to keep your software up to date.

Open the Terminal and run the update command:

sudo apt update	Copy
sudo apt full-upgrade	Copy
sudo reboot	Copy

Ensure your system is up-to-date.

4. Setting Screen Resolution

✔ Go to Preferences → Screen Configuration by clicking on the Raspberry icon.

✔ Select your display and set your desired resolution, for example, 1080p or 4K.

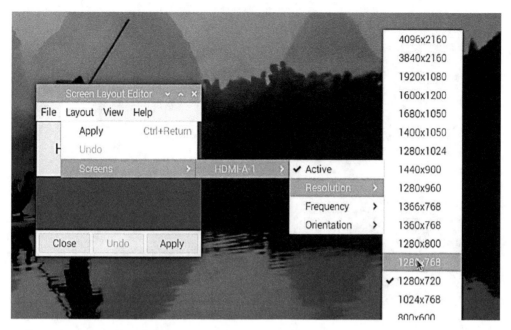

5. Installing Suggested Software

✔ Go to Preferences → Recommended Software from the menu.

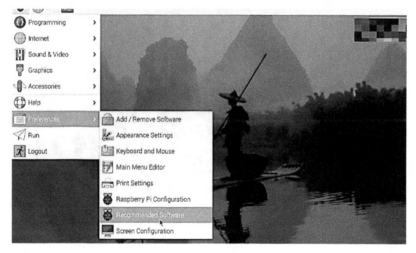

✔ Browse through the available apps, select those you need, and hit Apply so that they are automatically installed.

Quick Tips

✔ Safe Shutdown Methods

Press the power button twice.

Press the power button once, then select Shutdown.

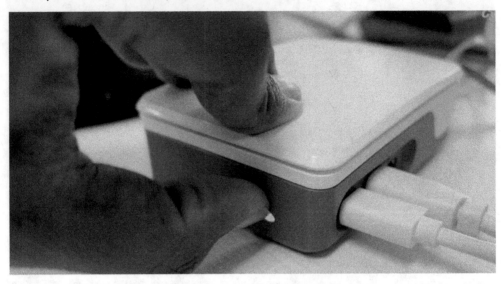

✔ Standard Shutdown

Click the Raspberry icon, go to Logout, and select Shutdown.

✔ Forced Shutdown (Use with Caution!)

Press and hold the power button for about 10 seconds. (Not recommended, as it may cause file corruption.)

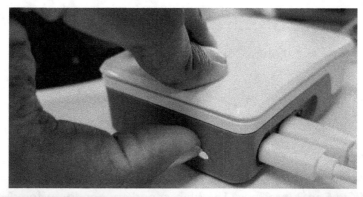

ESSENTIAL ACCESSORIES AND COMPONENTS

The Raspberry Pi 5 is the latest and most powerful model in the Raspberry Pi lineup, outperforming its predecessor, the Raspberry Pi 4. Available in 2GB, 4GB, 8GB, and 16GB RAM options, it serves as a capable, energy-efficient ARM-based desktop.

To fully unlock the potential of your Raspberry Pi 5, you'll need a few essential accessories. The Raspberry Pi ecosystem boasts an incredible variety of add-ons, including GPIO accessories that have been present from the very first models, when the board only had 26 GPIO pins. Although older ones are still usable, new HATs (Hardware Attached on Top) take advantage of the 40-pin GPIO, enabling exciting projects in robotics, IoT, machine learning, and even home server implementations. #### New Raspberry Pi 5 Accessories

With the introduction of the Raspberry Pi 5, a new line of accessories has been released, namely for the PCIe Gen 3 interface. The high-speed connection offers AI accelerators and high-speed storage solutions. Several cooling solutions and cases have also been introduced, including:

- Argon's THRML 60-RC
- ONE V3 M.2
- THRML Active Cooler

Certain of these accessories are already available, but others remain in the process of being approved.

Compatibility Considerations

Always double-check compatibility when purchasing accessories. While the GPIO layout is the same, some older HATs may require software workarounds since the RP1 chip accesses GPIO differently than older models. GPIO was accessed directly by the CPU previously. Check that your desired add-ons are well supported prior to purchasing them.

Essential Accessories for Your Raspberry Pi 5

As with any PC, the Raspberry Pi 5 requires essential peripherals such as a monitor, mouse, and keyboard. Or you can go for a headless installation, where you access it remotely from another device.

Following are the essentials required for a minimum installation:

✔ **microSD Card** – At least 16GB (32GB+ is recommended). The OS must be flashed onto the card from a PC, another Raspberry Pi, or a phone that has a microSD reader.

✔ **Power Supply** – A 5V, 5A power supply will be required for the Raspberry Pi 5. The official 27W power adapter is recommended to supply enough power for the board and accessories. For previous models:

Raspberry Pi 4: Power supply through USB-C (5V, 3A minimum)

Raspberry Pis previous to the Pi 4: Power supply via Micro USB (5V, 2.5A minimum)

Your power supply should provide enough headroom to power HATs and USB peripherals.

Other Accessories to Expand Capability

Besides the essentials, these accessories contribute to your Raspberry Pi enjoyment:

- **Cases** – Provide protection and better looks. Some cases have built-in cooling.

- **HATs (Add-on Boards)** – Add features, from motor control to LED displays.

- **Breakout Boards** – Provide more convenient access to GPIO pins, ideal for breadboarding and prototyping.

- **Camera Modules** – Connect to the dedicated camera port for photo-based, video streaming-based, or computer vision-based projects.

- **Heating Solutions** – Fans and Heatsinks help with heat control, especially for the Raspberry Pi 4 and 5.

- **Electronics Parts** – Transistors, motors, and sensors provide infinite project possibilities. Breadboards are essential for prototyping.

- **USB Storage** – The Raspberry Pi 4 and 5 can boot from USB SSDs or hard drives, with better performance and more storage.

THE BEST RASPBERRY PI ACCESSORIES YOU CAN BUY TODAY

Having the proper accessories for your Raspberry Pi can make all the difference in how well it performs and what you can use it for. Whether you desire better cooling, storage capacity, or functionality, there are a lot of fantastic add-ons to enhance your experience.

1. Compute Blade – Top Carrier Board for Compute Module 4

The Compute Blade is more than a carrier board—it's an ultra-high-performance "server on a stick" for blade server setups. It has a classy red anodized aluminum heat sink that holds the Compute Module 4 safely and in operation. Some of its key points are:

✔ M.2 NVMe slot for fast storage

✔ Gigabit Ethernet for reliable connectivity

✔ Power options via USB-C or Power over Ethernet (PoE)

✔ Integrated TPM for an added layer of security

Downside: Limited GPIO access, which might restrict certain projects.

2. Argon Neo Case – Best Raspberry Pi Case

If you want a small and efficient enclosure for your Raspberry Pi 4, the Argon Neo is the one. Made of aluminum, not only does it look good, but it also has passive cooling to keep temperatures cooler. Sliding magnetic lid offers easy access to GPIO pins when needed.

✔ Robust aluminum build

✔ Passive cooling for silent operation

✔ Easy GPIO access

Downside: You'll need to remove the cover to reach the pins.

3. Raspberry Pi High-Quality Camera – Best for Professional Photography

The Raspberry Pi High-Quality Camera is an excellent choice for photography and video projects, featuring a 12.3MP Sony IMX477R sensor for sharp, clear images. Its biggest advantage is interchangeable lenses, allowing for telephoto, macro, and other photography styles.

✔ Excellent image quality

✔ Supports multiple lenses

✔ Tripod mountable

Disadvantage: It's more expensive and comes without a lens.

4. Raspberry Pi Camera Module V3 – Best Budget Camera

For a decent but budget camera, the Raspberry Pi Camera Module V3 is a suitable option. It's compatible with all Raspberry Pi models and offers great image quality with HDR and autofocus.

✔ Compatible with all Raspberry Pi models

✔ Great image quality with HDR

✔ Affordable option

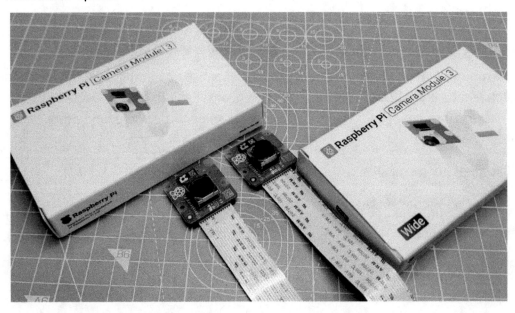

Downside: Slightly thicker than its predecessors and no screw mount.

5. Lenovo ThinkPad TrackPoint Keyboard II – Best Typing Keyboard for Raspberry Pi

A decent keyboard can make all the difference, and the Lenovo ThinkPad TrackPoint Keyboard II is no exception with one of the best typing experiences available. It's wireless, either through Bluetooth or a specific dongle, and has Lenovo's iconic TrackPoint for navigation.

✔ High-quality, comfortable typing

✔ Support for both Bluetooth and 2.4GHz wireless

✔ Long battery life

Disadvantage: It's very costly.

With a few accessories, your Raspberry Pi can be converted from a simple single-board computer into a powerful tool for all kinds of projects. Whether you're creating a server, a smart home gadget, or a photography setup, these accessories will help you get the most out of your Pi.

6. Raspberry Pi 5 Official Power Supply – Best Power Supply for Raspberry Pi

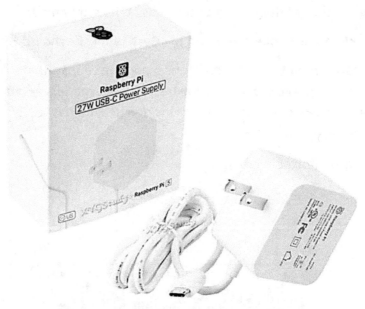

A good power supply for your Raspberry Pi 5 can't be beat with the official power supply. It's designed specifically for the Raspberry Pi 4 and 5, delivering a maximum power of 27W with a 5.1V/5A output. While your Raspberry Pi 5 doesn't need all of that power, it does offer add-on compatibility with devices like the new M.2 SSD HAT. And it even charges other devices like your Steam Deck or smartphone, due to PD compatibility. The only catch? No switch to turn it on and off, and not the cheapest, but a solid investment.

7. Pimoroni Explorer HAT Pro – Best Raspberry Pi HAT for Projects

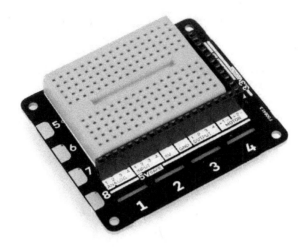

This add-on board is a fantastic tool for learning and experimentation. Whether you're an educator or a hobbyist, it provides an easy and safe way to interact with the Raspberry Pi's GPIO. It includes features like analog-to-digital conversion, motor control, LED lights, and a built-in breadboard for quick prototyping. While it doesn't support stacking with other HATs, its versatility makes it a great choice for creative projects.

8. Pimoroni Fan Shim – Best Raspberry Pi Cooling Solution

If keeping your Raspberry Pi cool is a priority for you, then the Pimoroni Fan Shim is a simple, no-nonsense solution.

Unlike the official Active Cooler, this fan is compatible with every model of Raspberry Pi and requires no configuration. It simply plugs into the GPIO and operates quietly to prevent your unit from heating up—even the Raspberry Pi 5! While it is slightly pricey in the US, it is a great choice to prevent thermal throttling and keep your projects running at their highest level.

9. Silicon Power 32GB 3D NAND microSD Card – Best Storage Option for Raspberry Pi

MicroSD cards have been the stock storage option for Raspberry Pi since 2014, but not all of them are performance heavyweights. That is where this Silicon Power card enters with its price to performance ratio balance that gives your Raspberry Pi project consistent performance. Boot times might not be the fastest, but this card offers consistent performance and maintains with the burden put on the Raspberry Pi 5.

10. GPIO Reference Board – Handy Accessory Perfection

Other than having committed the Raspberry Pi GPIO pin map to memory, a reference board is essential. Rather than forever referencing it online, this handy board slides straight over the GPIO pins with an easy-to-see pinout chart. It's particularly convenient for use in classrooms and makerspaces where ease of access to pin details is critical.

11. Micro HDMI to HDMI Adapters – Raspberry Pi 5 and 4 Must-Have

Since the Raspberry Pi 4 came with micro-HDMI ports, adapters have become an essential accessory. If you have already invested in standard HDMI cables, these adapters enable you to use them with your Raspberry Pi 4 or 5 without the need for new cables. They are simple, efficient, and make screen connectivity a breeze.

12.Freenove LCD 1602 Starter Kit – Best Kit for Learning Electronics

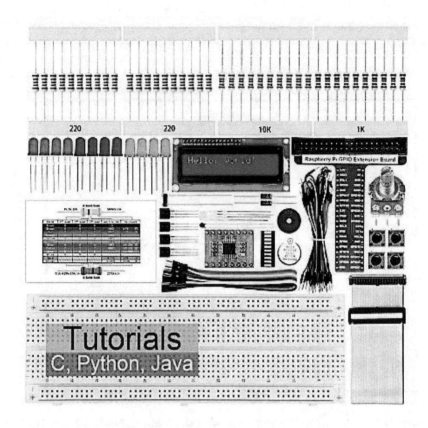

Getting into electronics might look intimidating, but this starter kit makes things easy. Everything you need—breadboards, jumper wires, sensors, and basic input/output devices—is included to start playing around with circuits. And with the online tutorials in C, Python, and Java provided, step-by-step guidelines are present, making it perfect for beginners and prototypers.

13. USB 3 MicroSD Card Reader – Best USB 3 Card Reader

If you have to read or write data from a microSD card for your Raspberry Pi, you'll need an external computer, and not all computers have internal microSD card readers. That's where these inexpensive USB 3 card readers come in handy. They support both micro and full-size SD cards and are simple to use with tools like Raspberry Pi Imager, Balena Etcher, and Rufus.

14. Raspberry Pi Zero Official Case – Top Case for Raspberry Pi Zero

While the Raspberry Pi 4 official case limits GPIO pin and camera port access, the Raspberry Pi Zero official case offers more flexibility. It comes with three removable lids:

one with a camera slot for uses like body cameras, another revealing the GPIO pins for easy prototyping, and a full lid for protection. It also comes in the Raspberry Pi Foundation's usual burgundy and white colorway. The catch is that you can't utilize both the camera cover and the GPIO at once.

15. Argon THRML 60-RC for Raspberry Pi 5 – Powerful Cooling with a Courageous Design

Cooling the Raspberry Pi 5 is vital for the best performance, and Argon Forty has delivered an incredibly effective cooling solution. This $20 cooler, housed in a silver, muscle-car-style case, features copper heat pipes, an aluminum heatsinks, and a substantial 60mm fan. While it is great at cooling, its size makes camera and display connectors hard to reach, and GPIO connections require a breakout board.

The cooling quality is superb. The Raspberry Pi 5 barely warmed up enough to start the fan during our tests, and even overclocking to 3 GHz, CPU temp was just 36.7°C. The fan is near silent at low speeds but can be noisy when running at maximum capacity. Although it features a large chunky appearance, this is an amazing value cooling solution for your Raspberry Pi 5.

CHAPTER 2

INSTALLING AND CONFIGURING THE PI OS

Make sure you have all the hardware before you begin installing your Raspberry Pi OS. The following is a list of what you'll need:

- **Raspberry Pi Board –** Any model from the Pi 2 upwards will be fine.

- **Power Supply –** Ensure it is the same voltage and amperage as your Raspberry Pi to prevent issues.

- **MicroSD Card –** At least 8GB (preferably a Class 10) for improved performance.

- **Accessories –** A protective case, an HDMI cable to send output to a monitor, and a USB mouse and keyboard to navigate.

- **Computer with an SD Card Reader –** This is used to flash the Raspberry Pi OS onto the microSD card before inserting it into your Pi.

Optional Extras: If you are upgrading your setup, you might also want:

- A USB hub to connect several peripherals in.

- An Ethernet cable for a safe wired internet connection.

- A breadboard and jumper wires to experiment with electronics.

Double-check that your power supply can provide the exact needs of your Raspberry Pi model to operate without problems and prevent any potential damage.

Raspberry Pi board with various components and accessories

Software Requirements

To do the Raspberry Pi OS tutorial, you will need a suitable Raspberry Pi model and a microSD card with at least 8GB storage capacity for the operating system. You will need a computer to download and install the OS image on the microSD card with the Raspberry Pi Imager tool, which is available for Windows, macOS, and Linux.

Once Raspberry Pi boots the OS, you shall utilize the in-built terminal and text editor for basic configuration and programming. Tutorial also contains procedure to adjust the system settings from the Raspberry Pi Configuration tool as well as accessing remotely with the help of SSH and VNC. Since Raspberry Pi OS does not contain optional software but required tools are installed pre-loaded, no software should be required for external purposes and hence it becomes very easy even for beginners.

INSTALLING RASPBERRY PI OS

Downloading the OS Image

To download the latest Raspberry Pi OS, visit the Raspberry Pi website at [Raspberry Pi OS Download] (https://www.raspberrypi.com/software/operating-systems/). There are multiple options, and the recommended one has a desktop environment, but the light version has no desktop. There's also a 64-bit option for advanced users. Choose the best version suitable for your needs, download the ZIP file, and unzip to get the OS image file (.img).

Writing the Image to the microSD Card

You'll require an instrument like Etcher, which accommodates Windows, macOS, and Linux, for writing the Raspberry Pi OS into your microSD card. You should start with downloading and setting up Etcher on your device. Open the application and select the Raspberry Pi OS image file you unzipped earlier. Insert your microSD card into your computer, select it as the target in Etcher, and then click on "Flash!" to begin the installation process. This should take a couple of minutes, depending on how large the image is and how fast your microSD card is.

After the flashing process is complete, Etcher will automatically verify the image to ensure it has been written correctly. After verifying, the microSD card can be inserted into your Raspberry Pi, and you can start discovering the Raspberry Pi OS.

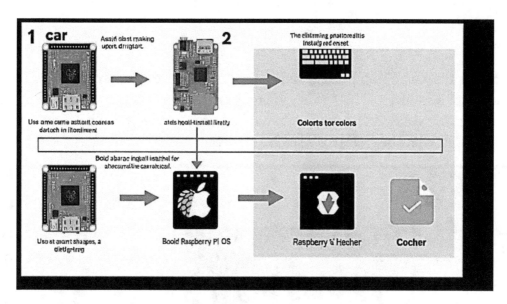

Step-by-step diagram of installing Raspberry Pi OS using Etcher

Booting Your Raspberry Pi

To boot your Raspberry Pi, begin by connecting the necessary accessories. Connect a USB mouse and keyboard, then connect your Raspberry Pi to a monitor or TV via an HDMI cable. Connect the microSD card with your Raspberry Pi OS into its respective slot on the board. Now that all is installed, insert the power supply into the Raspberry Pi micro-USB port and link it up to a power source. The Raspberry Pi will turn on automatically and begin booting. Within seconds, the Raspberry Pi OS desktop should be displayed on the screen. If the system will not boot as expected, ensure that all cables are correctly inserted, and insert the microSD card correctly with an appropriate operating system image. Once the booting process is successfully completed, your Raspberry Pi is ready to use, and you can start experimenting with its functions and projects.

SETTING UP YOUR RASPBERRY PI

Updating the System

The Raspberry Pi OS needs to be updated for security and performance. In order to update your system, proceed to the terminal and input `sudo apt update` to make a list of packages available update. After that, input `sudo apt upgrade` to upgrade software already installed to its latest version. Regular updating keeps your Raspberry Pi in top condition.

For updates that come with package dependencies for more complex ones, you can just use `sudo apt dist-upgrade`. Rebooting your Raspberry Pi after major updates ensures that all changes take effect. Staying up to date ensures you get the latest features, security updates, and bug fixes for a smooth experience.

Raspberry Pi desktop with key configuration settings

Customizing Your Raspberry Pi

Customizing the Raspberry Pi OS settings allows you to tailor the system to your needs. To alter the localization settings, open the Raspberry Pi Configuration tool from the home menu. From the "Localisation" page, you can alter the language, timezone, keyboard layout, and Wi-Fi country settings based on your location and preference.

If your keyboard layout is not compatible with your installation, select the correct one among those provided. This will ensure that the keys you type are equal to the characters displayed on the screen.

To connect to a Wi-Fi network, click on the network icon in the top-right corner of the screen, choose your preferred network, and enter the password when asked. Your Raspberry Pi will then be connected.

You can also dig into more settings, for example, changing the audio output, changing the resolution of the display, or enabling remote access via SSH or VNC. Configuring these options will take some time to set up, but it will give a more streamlined and user-friendly experience.

INSTALLING USEFUL SOFTWARE

Once you have your Raspberry Pi set up, you can install new software to add to its capabilities. The built-in package manager, "apt," makes it straightforward. Start by opening a terminal and updating the list of packages with `sudo apt update`, followed by upgrading existing software with `sudo apt upgrade`.

For coding and development, you might be interested in installing a text editor like Visual Studio Code (`sudo apt install code`) or Sublime Text. For web development, you can install Apache, PHP, and MySQL with `sudo apt install apache2 php mysql-server`.

Python is in fact preinstalled on Raspberry Pi OS, though you can always check to have the latest installed by using the command `sudo apt install python3`. When you do your programming using a different language, like Java or Node.js, you can fetch those by simply using their corresponding `apt` commands.

Version control is essential to software projects, so the installation of Git (`sudo apt install git`) is convenient. Convenient are also `htop` for displaying system usage of resources (`sudo apt install htop`) and VNC for remote desktop display (`sudo apt install realvnc-vnc-server`).

The Raspberry Pi community provides an infinite number of software options, so make sure to check out the official repositories and web forums for searching for tools that suit your projects.

Beginning Your Raspberry Pi Projects

As a beginner, if you are new to Raspberry Pi, some of the simplest projects that you can try are as follows:

- **Retro Gaming Console –** Use RetroPie to convert your Raspberry Pi into an old-school console with support for a large variety of retro games.

- **Media Center** – Install Kodi to set up a home media server that streams movies, TV shows, and music.
- **Web Server** – Use Apache, PHP, and MySQL to have an inexpensive web hosting environment.
- **Home Automation Hub** – Use platforms like Home Assistant or OpenHAB to automate and control smart devices in your home.

Expanding Your Knowledge

To keep on building your Raspberry Pi skills, look to the official Raspberry Pi site for documentation, tutorials, and online courses. You can also join communities such as the Raspberry Pi Forums and Reddit's r/raspberry_pi to connect with other enthusiasts, get answers, and share your projects. Sites such as Instructables and The MagPi magazine provide step-by-step guides and inspiration for new projects.

Wrapping Up

With the use of this tutorial, you now have a working Raspberry Pi with an OS installed, customized settings, and the required software. From here, you can expand further on new projects and applications, be it building a media server, making a gaming console, or experimenting with IoT devices. With an active community and endless possibilities, your Raspberry Pi journey has begun.

CHOOSING THE RIGHT OPERATING SYSTEM

The Raspberry Pi is a small but powerful computer used for all types of projects—home automation and media center to robots and education. But to achieve the best performance from your Raspberry Pi, you need to choose the right file system.

A file system is where your data gets stored and kept on an SD card or USB drive. The right selection ensures speed, dependability, and compatibility for your specific project. This tutorial discusses the options and helps you make the best decision for your setup.

What Is a File System?

Think of a file system as a librarian who holds books (your files) on shelves (your storage). A librarian organizes books by name and author, and a file system organizes files, holds them in place, and accesses them when needed.

Without a good file system, your Raspberry Pi would be unaware of the location of your files or how to access them efficiently.

FIVE THINGS TO CONSIDER WHEN CHOOSING A FILE SYSTEM

Not all file systems are created equal. Here are five things to keep in mind:

1. Performance

If your work is video editing, gaming, or dealing with large files, you need an efficient and fast file system. Some are better for always editing files, and others are better for reading or writing large amounts of data.

2. Reliability & Data Protection

Data corruption may occur as a result of sudden power failures or system crashes. Certain file systems employ journaling (which keeps track of file modifications) or checksums (which check data integrity) to assist in recovering files in case something goes amiss. If data protection is a concern, choose a file system that includes built-in protection.

3. Compatibility

Your file system needs to be compatible not just with Raspberry Pi OS, but with whatever device you're using. For example, if you wish to move files between your Raspberry Pi and a Windows machine, choose a format that both computers recognize.

4. Features & Flexibility

Other file systems offer some additional advantages like encryption (for safety), compression (to save space), or deduplication (to eliminate redundant files). Depending on your project, these features might prove useful.

5. Ease of Use

If you are new to it, you will want a file system that's simple to install and manage. More advanced users might want one with more control but at the cost of having to work with command-line utilities.

Selecting the Right One

There is no single solution that fits all. The best file system depends on how you plan to utilize your Raspberry Pi. Consider what matters most—speed, security, compatibility, or ease of use—and choose accordingly.

By choosing the right file system, you'll be able to keep your Raspberry Pi running smoothly and efficiently, no matter what you're doing!

Choosing the Best File System for Your Raspberry Pi

Having covered the key considerations, let's examine some of the most widely used file systems and their best use cases for Raspberry Pi.

1. FAT32 – Universal Compatibility, but Limited Features

FAT32 is a very old and broadly supported file system. It reads and writes perfectly under Windows, macOS, and Linux and is an excellent choice if you must share files with other devices.

Advantages:

- o Functions on nearly any device or OS

- o Easy to use and simple

Disadvantages:

4GB maximum file size limit

Does not provide support for advanced features like journaling and file permissions

Best For:

If you're using your Raspberry Pi as a basic media player or for simple file sharing, FAT32 is perfect since it has universal compatibility.

2. exFAT – FAT32 with Large File Support Enhancement

exFAT is a variant of FAT32 that removes the 4GB file size limit and is also faster. It's still very compatible with Windows and macOS, but some versions of Linux will require extra setup to get it working.

Pros:

- Very large file sizes are supported

- Good performance on a variety of operating systems

Cons:

- Lack of journaling means data corruption is possible on crashes
- Requires additional software on some Linux systems

Best For:

If you need to transfer large media files (e.g., videos) back and forth between your Raspberry Pi and other computers, exFAT is a suitable option.

3. ext4 – The Default and Stable Linux Option

ext4 is the most popular file system for Linux operating systems, such as Raspberry Pi OS. It provides excellent reliability, performance, and large file support. As it has journaling included, it also prevents file corruption during a crash or power failure.

Pros:

- Excellent performance and reliability
- Large file and volume storage support
- Journaling prevents file corruption

Cons:

Primarily Linux-based (not natively supported by Windows or macOS)

Best For:

If you are running Raspberry Pi OS and require a high-performance, stable file system, ext4 is the ideal choice—especially for projects involving heavy file access or those that demand strong data integrity.

4. Btrfs – Advanced Features for Power Users

Btrfs is a more modern file system that goes beyond just the normal file storage. It includes snapshots, compression, and deduplication of data natively and would be ideal for backup systems or projects that require extra data safeguarding.

Pros:

- Snapshots supported for easy backups
- Built-in file compression and deduplication
- Strong data integrity features

Cons:

- More difficult to set up and maintain compared to ext4
- Consumes more system resources

Best For:

Btrfs is an excellent choice if you're handling sensitive data, version control, or you want to automate backups.

5. XFS – Designed for High Performance and Large Data

XFS is a high-performance file system that is optimized for large files and large datasets. It's typically used in professional server platforms and applications that need fast access to data.

Pros:

- Handles large files and large data efficiently
- Suitable for performance-critical apps

Cons:

- Not ideal for small projects
- Does not support shrinking of the file system

Best For:

If your Raspberry Pi is handling large files—such as video editing, scientific computing, or use as a file server—XFS may be a suitable choice.

Choosing the Best File System for Your Project

The best file system will depend on your intended use of the Raspberry Pi. Here's a quick guide to help you decide:

- For general Raspberry Pi OS usage: Keep to ext4 for performance and stability.
- For cross-operating system file sharing: Use exFAT for large files or FAT32 for basic compatibility.
- For data backup and more sophisticated storage management: Investigate Btrfs for snapshotting and data integrity.
- For large datasets and high-performance applications: XFS is a great choice.

71

By matching your file system to your project's needs, you'll ensure better performance, reliability, and ease of use on your Raspberry Pi.

Choosing the Right Operating System for Your Raspberry Pi 5

If you're wondering which operating system (OS) is best for your Raspberry Pi 5—whether for daily use or a specific project—there are several options to consider.

Raspberry Pi OS – The Reliable Default

Raspberry Pi OS is the official operating system designed specifically for Raspberry Pi devices. It's built for stability, runs smoothly, and includes all the essential tools for general computing and programming. If you're looking for a straightforward and optimized experience, this is a solid choice.

That said, if you prefer a more modern design or need better multitasking features, you might want to explore other options.

Ubuntu 23.10 (Mantic Minotaur) – A Sleek Alternative

For those who want a more refined and professional-looking OS, Ubuntu 23.10 could be a great fit. It offers:

- A polished interface with a built-in dock for easy navigation
- Smooth high-quality video streaming
- More customization options for users who like to tweak their settings

Ubuntu handles multitasking differently from Raspberry Pi OS, so if you want more flexibility in managing your apps, it might be the better choice.

Ultimately, the best OS for your Raspberry Pi depends on what you need—whether it's simplicity, performance, or advanced customization.

RASPBERRY PI OPERATING SYSTEMS

Raspberry Pi 5 has an impressive array of operating systems, all with varying sets of applications. Whether you are using it for general usage, media streaming, security scanning, or specific applications, there is an OS available to meet your needs.

1. Raspberry Pi OS – The Official and Reliable Choice

Originally referred to as Raspbian, Raspberry Pi OS is the official operating system across all Raspberry Pi boards. Designed on Debian, it offers a stable and secure environment, which is optimized for Raspberry Pi hardware. Tuned to deliver a smooth experience, particularly on Raspberry Pi 5, this OS supports graphical programs and multimedia file playback.

It has included programming tools, and it is a good fit for learning, hobby development, and coding. But its plain look and limited multitasking features might not appeal to those seeking a more modern feel. Updates to Raspberry Pi OS still revolve around performance and stability.

2. Ubuntu 23.10 (Mantic Minotaur) – A Sleek and Versatile Alternative

Ubuntu 23.10 sports a neater and more professional-appearing desktop than Raspberry Pi OS. Among the best features are:

- A responsive, user-friendly desktop with a dock for instant program access
- Enhanced performance for tasks like 1080p media streaming
- A new App Center for simple management of software packages
- GNOME 45, which is easier to use and provides a modern interface

Ubuntu is a great choice for those who want more control over their settings and a refined desktop environment.

3. Armbian – Lightweight and Efficient

Armbian is a Debian-based OS for ARM development boards like the Raspberry Pi 5. It features:

- A feature-rich but minimalistic interface with XFCE for a light experience
- A BASH shell for power users who like the command line
- A simplified setup process with Debian tools for easy setup

Although lightweight and ARM hardware highly optimized, media streaming may not be as smooth as other distributions due to less optimization for some codecs.

4. OpenFyde – A Web-Focused Chromium OS

Built on Chromium OS, OpenFyde is perfect for those who appreciate web-based applications, streaming media over the internet, and cloud applications. Its advantages are:

- A lean build optimized for surfing and internet applications

- A build that accommodates custom cloud applications

- Open-source flexibility, whereby it can be customized to specs

Since OpenFyde is intended for use online, it's an excellent option for users who want a Chromium OS-based experience on their Raspberry Pi 5.

5. Kali Linux – The Cybersecurity Go-To OS

Kali Linux is a specialized OS for ethical hacking, penetration testing, and cybersecurity research. It comes with a huge collection of security tools for:

- Vulnerability analysis

- Network security testing

- Digital forensics

If cybersecurity is your thing, Kali Linux provides a professional set of tools to assist with the testing and safeguarding of networks and systems.

6. Specialized Operating Systems – For Specific Unique Requirements

There are OS versions as well that have been developed for unique requirements, i.e.:

- LibreELEC – Light OS for Kodi-based media centers

- Recalbox – Ideal for retro gaming

- FullPageOS – Suitable for digital signage use cases

- Moodlebox – A great tool for learning environments

- Lumina – A specialist OS for music enthusiasts

These niche operating systems are created for specific purposes, offering the top-of-the-line experiences for entertainment, learning, or automation projects.

7. Android by Emteria – Bringing Mobile Apps to Raspberry Pi

For users looking for an Android experience on Raspberry Pi 5, Android by Emteria provides:

- A comfortable mobile interface

- Ability to access Android apps and services
- Touchscreen support for applications needing a mobile-like user experience

While there is a free starter plan, users must sign up to use it. This OS is especially handy for app development, media consumption, or projects that need a touch-based interface.

Selecting the Best OS for Your Raspberry Pi 5

With so many choices, the best OS is based on your individual needs:

- General coding & computing? → Ubuntu or Raspberry Pi OS
- Media web browsing & streaming? → OpenFyde or Ubuntu
- Penetration testing & cybersecurity? → Kali Linux
- Lightweight & minimalist? → Armbian
- Special purposes? → Moodlebox, LibreELEC, or Recalbox
- Android application compatibility? → Android by Emteria

Every operating system possesses its own virtues, and you can customize your Raspberry Pi 5 experience to suit your demands and desires.

BASIC SYSTEM SETTINGS AND UPDATES

Keeping your Raspberry Pi OS updated is like giving it a security boost. Just like your phone or computer needs updates to stay protected, your Raspberry Pi does too—especially if you access it remotely via SSH or VNC. Regular updates fix vulnerabilities and keep your device safe from potential threats. Think of it as a regular check-up to keep everything running smoothly.

If you're using the official Raspberry Pi OS, updating is quick and easy. But don't underestimate its importance! If you work with sensitive data or use Python packages, staying up to date is essential to avoid security risks.

Better Performance with Updates

Updating doesn't just improve security—it also enhances your Raspberry Pi's performance. Each update fine-tunes the system, making everything run faster and more efficiently. From optimizing the Linux kernel to improving firmware, these updates help your Raspberry Pi run smoother. Even simple things, like audio over HDMI, can see noticeable improvements!

Many Raspberry Pi users (around 80%) update their systems regularly because they've experienced the difference it makes. A well-maintained OS ensures your device works at its best.

Access New Features and Stay Compatible

Updates bring more than just fixes—they introduce new features and better functionality. Whether it's improved video playback, support for new hardware, or performance enhancements, every update brings something valuable.

Keeping your OS up to date also ensures compatibility with the latest software, peripherals, and Python libraries. Just like updating your smartphone to support new apps, updating your Raspberry Pi lets you use the latest tools and features without compatibility issues.

Preparing for an Update

Before updating your Raspberry Pi, take a few simple steps to make the process smooth:

✔ Back Up Your Data – Save important files to an external drive or cloud storage. If you've made any system customizations, write them down so you can restore them if needed. Tools like `rsync` or `dd` can help with backups.

✔ Check Your OS Version – Run `cat /etc/os-release` in the terminal to see your current version. Compare it with the latest release to see if an update is needed.

✔ Ensure a Stable Internet Connection – A strong Wi-Fi or Ethernet connection is crucial for downloading updates without interruptions. You can test your connection using `ping google.com`. If there are any issues, fix them before starting the update.

HOW TO UPDATE YOUR RASPBERRY PI

If you're running an older version like Stretch, you'll need to update in stages rather than jumping straight to the latest version (Bookworm). The correct order is:

1. Stretch → Buster

2. Buster → Bullseye

3. Bullseye → Bookworm

Use `sudo apt update` regularly to keep your software, firmware, and Linux kernel up to date. If you're updating via SSH, consider using the `screen` utility to prevent disruptions if the connection drops.

Most updates (about 90%) go smoothly, but it's always good to be prepared for any issues. Regular updates keep your Raspberry Pi secure, improve its performance, and ensure you have access to the latest features—so don't skip them!

Keeping Your Raspberry Pi OS Up to Date

Updating your Raspberry Pi's operating system is essential for keeping it running smoothly and securely. Fortunately, the process is straightforward, especially if you're using the official Raspberry Pi OS. Since it's built on Debian (similar to Ubuntu Server), managing updates is simple and familiar.

Step 1: Open the Terminal

To begin, open the terminal. If you're using the Raspberry Pi desktop, click the terminal icon. If you're accessing it remotely, connect via SSH.

Learning a few basic terminal commands can make things easier. You can also use the shortcut CTRL + ALT + T to open the terminal quickly.

Make sure you're logged in as a user with root privileges, as you'll need them to run system updates.

Step 2: Update Software Packages

First, refresh the package list by running:

```bash
sudo apt update
```

This ensures your system knows about the latest available software versions. Next, upgrade your installed packages with:

```bash
sudo apt upgrade -y
```

The -y flag automatically approves the updates, saving you time. Watch the terminal for any messages that might need your attention.

For a more thorough update that also handles dependencies, run:

```bash
sudo apt dist-upgrade
```

Step 3: Upgrade to the Latest OS Version

If you want to upgrade to a newer version of Raspberry Pi OS, you'll need to edit the system's sources list.

1. Open the sources list file:

```bash
sudo nano /etc/apt/sources.list
```

2. Find the current OS version name (e.g., "bullseye") and replace it with the latest one (e.g., "bookworm").

3. Save your changes and exit the editor.

4. Update and upgrade your system again:

```bash
```

```
sudo apt update && sudo apt upgrade
```
```

This process may take around 10–15 minutes, depending on your internet speed.

### Step 4: Restart Your Raspberry Pi

Once the updates are complete, restart your device to apply the changes:

```bash

sudo reboot

```

After rebooting, check your OS version to confirm that the update was successful. Also, test your apps to make sure everything is working correctly.

To update the bootloader to the latest preview version, use:

```bash

sudo rpi-update

```

This usually happens automatically once the update is stable in the Raspberry Pi package repository.

Managing Software on Raspberry Pi with APT

If you use a Raspberry Pi regularly, it helps to know how to install and manage software efficiently. The Advanced Package Tool (APT) is built into Raspberry Pi OS and makes it easy to install, update, and remove applications, as well as update the Linux kernel and firmware.

Since APT is specifically optimized for Raspberry Pi OS, about 90% of users rely on it for software management.

Installing New Software

Looking to add new functionality to your Raspberry Pi? Whether you need a media server, a coding environment, or other tools, you can install software using:

```bash

sudo apt install [package_name]
```
```

```
```

For example, to install the Apache web server, enter:

```bash
sudo apt install apache2
```

You can explore different software options in available repositories and find programs designed specifically for Raspberry Pi OS. Keeping track of installed packages helps you manage your system efficiently.

Removing Unneeded Software

Over time, you might install programs that you no longer need. To see a list of installed software, run:

```bash
dpkg --get-selections
```

To remove a package, use:

```bash
sudo apt remove [package_name]
```

If you also want to delete its configuration files, run:

```bash
sudo apt purge [package_name]
```

Regularly cleaning up unused software helps keep your Raspberry Pi running efficiently—just like keeping your workspace organized!

Clearing Out Space on Your Raspberry Pi

Since Raspberry Pi has limited space, it needs to be cleaned. Here is how you can clear out space:

Clear out unwanted files: Use `sudo apt autoremove` to clear out software that you no longer use, like cleaning out old trash.

Empty package files: Clean out old downloads and free up additional space using `sudo apt autoclean`.

Inspect your storage: Check out how much space is left by using `df -h`.

Identify big files: A program such as `ncdu` provides you with a clear picture of what is occupying the most room, making it simpler to choose what to remove.

UPDATING YOUR RASPBERRY PI

It is necessary to update your Raspberry Pi firmware in order to keep it running smoothly and to ensure it is compatible with newer software. Firmware can be described as the brain that dictates how the hardware works. Without updates, your system will decay or even become incompatible with newer functionality.

To update, simply enter:

```bash
sudo rpi-update
```

```
```

This pulls the latest firmware directly from the official Raspberry Pi servers, ensuring your system stays current. Regular updates improve performance, fix bugs, and keep everything running efficiently.

Checking Your Firmware Version

Before updating, it's helpful to check which firmware version your Raspberry Pi is running. Use this command:

```bash
vcgencmd version
```

This will show your current firmware version. Compare it with the latest version listed on the Raspberry Pi website to see if an update is needed.

Also, make sure your firmware is compatible with your operating system. For instance, if you're using a Raspberry Pi 5, it might not work with a new OS like Bullseye without a few adjustments.

Installing the Latest Firmware

To upgrade to the latest firmware, run:

```bash
sudo rpi-update
```

Your Raspberry Pi will download and install the update. Once it is done, restart your device to apply the changes:

```bash
sudo reboot
```

Once you've rebooted, check the firmware version again to confirm the update took place. If the new version causes issues, you can roll back to a stable release at any time.

Update Troubleshooting Issues

If something goes wrong during updating, apply these steps of troubleshooting:

Troubleshooting Network Issues

Verify your connections: Make sure your Raspberry Pi is properly connected to the internet.

Restart your router: Restarting sometimes may help fix connectivity problems.

Verify network settings: Use `ifconfig` to ensure your Raspberry Pi has the correct network details.

Try another network: Switching Wi-Fi or using a different connection can debug the issue.

Fixing Package Installation Issues

- **Repair broken installations:** Run `sudo apt --fix-broken install` to repair any broken updates.
- **Check for error messages:** The terminal will typically give hints as to what went wrong.
- **Delete old files**: Run `sudo apt clean` to remove old package files and avoid conflicts.
- **Update again**: Having fixed the issues, run the update process again.

Fixing Boot Issues

Inspect system logs: Use `dmesg` or `journalctl` to know why your Raspberry Pi will not boot properly.

Rollback updates: If the most recent firmware is not functional, you may revert to a prior version.

Use recovery mode: This assists in debugging if your Raspberry Pi cannot boot.

Restore from backup: Only as a final option, returning to a backup can save you from facing major problems.

By keeping your Raspberry Pi clean, updated, and well-maintained, you'll ensure it runs smoothly and stays compatible with the latest software.

MANUALLY UPDATING THE RASPBERRY PI BOOTLOADER

Upgrading the bootloader on your Raspberry Pi may seem techie, but it's quite easy. The bootloader is like the conductor of an orchestra—only when it gets all the hardware pieces ready will your operating system begin. Updating it keeps the system stable and avoids booting problems that will render your Pi useless.

The firmware is what carries out this task. When you upgrade the firmware, you'll need a suitable bootloader to assist it all to function well.

What the Bootloader Does

Bootloader is responsible for booting your Raspberry Pi's hardware and loading the operating system. If it is not updated, you could experience failures at boot, crashes, or slowness. Keeping it up to date ensures that your system stays stable and responsive.

Manually Updating the Bootloader

While automatic updates usually handle this, sometimes you'll need to update it manually. Here's how to do it step by step:

1. Download the Latest Bootloader Files – Visit the official Raspberry Pi website and grab the most recent bootloader update. This ensures you're working with the newest version.

2. Create an SD Card – Download an application like balenaEtcher and use it to flash the bootloader files onto a fresh SD card. Make sure to back up any precious data, as this will erase existing content.

3. Insert the SD Card and Power On – Put your revised SD card into your Raspberry Pi and turn it on. The Raspberry Pi Imager can guide you through this, although you will get messages that your data can be lost—just another reason why backups are useful!

4. Watch for Update Process – The update itself will be approximately 30 seconds long. You can see on an attached HDMI display a green box flashing while that is happening that suggests the update. When the process finishes, your Raspberry Pi will shut down and immediately boot back up in the same manner.

The Raspberry Pi Imager is the easiest way of updating your bootloader, but manually you can via SSH or raspi-config if that suits you better. Done correctly, this has a 90% success rate for your Raspberry Pi to boot nicely.

Now that you know how to update your Raspberry Pi OS, firmware, and bootloader, you're ready to keep your system purring like a kitten. Updates not only speed up the system but also improve it from a security standpoint. If you ever run into issues, now you have the troubleshooting skills to handle them like a pro.

Want to know more? Check out more guides and discover new ways to get the best out of your Raspberry Pi. Your journey's just beginning—go and create some magic!

Frequently Asked Questions

1. Why should I update my Raspberry Pi OS?

Updating your system ensures security, stability, and better performance. Each update fixes bugs, patches vulnerabilities, and enhances software compatibility—especially for running Python packages and tools.

2. How do I prepare an update?

Prior to doing that, save your essential files. Ensure your Raspberry Pi is plugged into a stable internet, is well-powered, and has enough storage space to go through the update process without interruption.

3. How do I upgrade the Raspberry Pi OS?

Launch the terminal and enter:

```sh
sudo apt update && sudo apt full-upgrade -y
```

This updates your list of packages and upgrades all software installed. Reboot your Raspberry Pi after the update is finished to make the changes active.

4. How do I use APT for managing software packages?

- Enter `sudo apt update` to refresh the package list.

- Update installed packages with available updates using `sudo apt upgrade`.

- Install a specific package with `sudo apt install [package_name]`.

5. How do I update the Raspberry Pi firmware?

Run the following command in the terminal:

```sh
sudo rpi-update
```

Once updated, restart your Raspberry Pi so that the new firmware can take effect.

6. What should I do if I face update problems?

- Make sure you have a stable internet connection and enough storage space.

- Check error messages for clues about what is wrong.

- Visit the Raspberry Pi forums for troubleshooting advice or seek a professional if needed.

7. How do I manually update the bootloader?

- Insert the microSD card into your computer.

- Copy the new bootloader file to the boot partition.

- Reinsert the card into your Raspberry Pi and reboot to complete the update.

CHAPTER 3

EXPLORING GPIO AND HARDWARE PROJECTS

The Raspberry Pi 5 is more powerful than its predecessors, but it also comes with some changes—especially in how the GPIO (General Purpose Input/Output) functions. While the 40-pin GPIO layout remains the same, it now connects through the new RP1 southbridge chip. This affects how we write code to control it.

Previously, most projects used the `RPi.GPIO` library, a widely adopted community project by Ben Croston. However, due to changes in how the GPIO pins are mapped in memory, `RPi.GPIO` no longer works on the Raspberry Pi 5. Instead, we need to use a different library called `libgpiod`.

What is `libgpiod`?

`libgpiod`, specifically the `python3-gpiod` module, is a Python library that lets us control the GPIO pins on the Raspberry Pi 5. It works similarly to `RPi.GPIO` in that we must configure pins before using them. However, `gpiod` serves as a middle layer between Python and the hardware.

If you're new to working with the GPIO, a simpler option is `GPIO Zero`, a beginner-friendly library created by Ben Nuttall and Dave Jones, which also supports the Raspberry Pi 5.

Simple Raspberry Pi 5 GPIO Projects

To better understand how `gpiod` works, we'll walk through two basic projects:

1. Blinking an LED (output)

2. Controlling an LED with a button (input/output)

What You'll Need

- Raspberry Pi 5
- Breadboard
- 4 male-to-female jumper wires
- 1 LED
- 100-ohm resistor (Brown-Black-Brown-Gold)
- Push button

Project 1: Making an LED Blink

Whenever you learn a new programming language, the first project is usually displaying "Hello, World!" In electronics, the equivalent is making an LED blink.

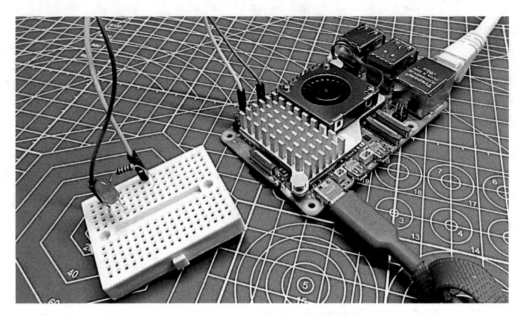

Setting Up the Circuit

The wiring is simple:

- Connect the longer leg of the LED (anode) to GPIO 17 using a jumper wire.

- Connect the shorter leg (cathode) to GND (ground) through a 100-ohm resistor.

- If you don't have a 100-ohm resistor, you can use one between 100 and 330 ohms (color code: Orange-Orange-Brown-Gold).

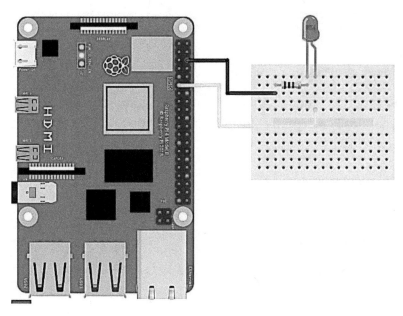

Making an LED Blink with Python on Raspberry Pi 5

Now that we've got our hardware set up, let's write a simple Python program to make the LED blink.

Step 1: Open Thonny and Import Necessary Modules

First, open Thonny, the built-in Python editor on Raspberry Pi. Then, import the required modules:

- `gpiod` – This lets us control and interact with the GPIO pins.

- `time` – This allows us to add delays in the program.

```python
import gpiod
import time
```

Step 2: Define the GPIO Pin for the LED

We need to assign a pin number for our LED. We'll use GPIO 17, following the Broadcom pin numbering system, which is the standard for Raspberry Pi.

```python
```

```
LED_PIN = 17
```

Step 3: Specify the GPIO Chip

Unlike older Raspberry Pi models that used a single `gpiomem` device, the Raspberry Pi 5 now uses dynamically assigned chips. The correct one for GPIO control is gpiochip4.

```python
chip = gpiod.Chip('gpiochip4')
```

Step 4: Create a Reference to the LED Pin

In `gpiod`, GPIO pins are called "lines." We need to tell the program which pin we're working with.

```python
led_line = chip.get_line(LED_PIN)
```

Step 5: Set the LED as an Output

Before we can turn the LED on or off, we need to configure its pin as an output so it can send electrical signals.

```python
led_line.request(consumer="LED", type=gpiod.LINE_REQ_DIR_OUT)
```

Step 6: Create a Loop to Blink the LED

We'll use a while loop to repeatedly turn the LED on and off. The `try` block ensures the code keeps running until we stop it manually.

```python
try:
    while True:
```

Step 7: Turn the LED On for One Second

By setting the pin's value to 1, we turn the LED on. The `time.sleep(1)` command keeps it on for one second.

```python
led_line.set_value(1)
time.sleep(1)
```

Step 8: Turn the LED Off for One Second

Setting the pin's value to 0 turns the LED off, followed by another one-second pause.

```python
led_line.set_value(0)
time.sleep(1)
```

Step 9: Ensure Proper Cleanup

Unlike some other libraries, `gpiod` requires us to release the GPIO pin when stopping the program. This prevents issues when running the code again later.

```python
finally:
led_line.release()
```

Step 10: Save and Run the Program

1. Save the file as blinky.py.

2. Click Run in Thonny, and the LED will start blinking every second.

3. To stop the program, press CTRL + C or click Stop in Thonny.

That's it! You've now successfully programmed your Raspberry Pi 5 to control an LED using Python.

Project 1: Complete Code Listing

```
1   import gpiod
2   import time
3   LED_PIN = 17
4   chip = gpiod.Chip('gpiochip4')
5   led_line = chip.get_line(LED_PIN)
6   led_line.request(consumer="LED", type=gpiod.LINE_REQ_DIR_OUT)
7   try:
8       while True:
9           led_line.set_value(1)
10          time.sleep(1)
11          led_line.set_value(0)
12          time.sleep(1)
13  finally:
14      led_line.release()
```

PROJECT 2: INPUT, REACT TO USER INPUT

After getting a blinking LED to work, the next step is learning how to handle inputs using a button.

In this example, we'll connect a button to the Raspberry Pi. One side of the button will be attached to a GPIO pin, while the other side will be connected to 3.3V (3V3) power.

By default, the GPIO pin isn't receiving power, so its state is 0 (False, Low).

When you press the button, it completes the circuit by linking the 3.3V pin to the GPIO pin, changing its state to 1 (True, High).

Our Python code will detect this change and respond accordingly. To set this up, you only need a button and two jumper wires.

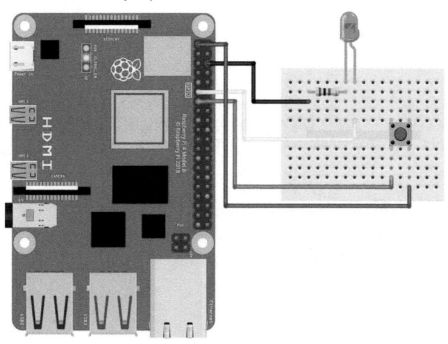

Creating a Button-Controlled LED Program for Raspberry Pi 5

Below is a basic Python program you can create to turn an LED on when you press a button and turn it off when you release the button.

✔ **Step 1: Open Thonny and import two simple modules:**

- gpiod (to read and control GPIO pins)
- time (to include pauses in the code)

```python
import gpiod
import time
```

✔️ **Step 2:** Declare the GPIO pins of the LED and button through the creation of two variables:

- The LED is on GPIO 17

- The button is connected to GPIO 27 (adjacent to GPIO 17)

```python
LED_PIN = 17
BUTTON_PIN = 27
```

✔️ **Step 3**: Let the program know where to find the GPIO pins. The Raspberry Pi 5, using the RP1 chip, uses `gpiochip4` to manage GPIO processes.

```python
chip = gpiod.Chip('gpiochip4')
```

✔️ **Step 4**: Use variables to reference the LED and button pins. The gpiod module refers to GPIO pins as "lines."

```python
led_line = chip.get_line(LED_PIN)
button_line = chip.get_line(BUTTON_PIN)
```

✔️ **Step 5: Initialize the GPIO pins:**

Configure the LED pin as an output (so it can turn on and off).

Configure the button pin as an input (so it can detect when the button is pressed).

```python
led_line.request(consumer="LED", type=gpiod.LINE_REQ_DIR_OUT)
button_line.request(consumer="Button", type=gpiod.LINE_REQ_DIR_IN)
```

✔️ **Step 6:** Create a loop that constantly monitors if the button is pressed. The try-except block enables the program to handle interruptions and clean up when quitting.

```python
try:
    while True:
        # Read the button's current state
```

button_state = button_line.get_value()
    # If button is pressed (state = 1), the LED is ON
    if button_state == 1:
        led_line.set_value(1)
# Otherwise, switch off the LED
        else:
            led_line.set_value(0)
```

✔️ **Step 7:** Free GPIO resources when the script finishes. This prevents errors on the next run of the script.

```python
finally:
    led_line.release()
    button_line.release()
```

✔️ **Step 8:** Save the file as button-press.py and click Run to test it out.

- Press the button → The LED becomes on.
- Release the button → The LED becomes off.
- Press CTRL + C or click Stop to terminate the program.

This simple project encompasses the fundamentals of reading inputs and controlling outputs on the Raspberry Pi 5!
```

PROJECT 2: COMPLETE CODE LISTING

```
1   import gpiod
2   LED_PIN = 17
3   BUTTON_PIN = 27
4   chip = gpiod.Chip('gpiochip4')
5   led_line = chip.get_line(LED_PIN)
6   button_line = chip.get_line(BUTTON_PIN)
7   led_line.request(consumer="LED", type=gpiod.LINE_REQ_DIR_OUT)
8   button_line.request(consumer="Button", type=gpiod.LINE_REQ_DIR
9   try:
10      while True:
11          button_state = button_line.get_value()
12          if button_state == 1:
13              led_line.set_value(1)
14          else:
15              led_line.set_value(0)
16  finally:
17      led_line.release()
18  button_line.release()
```

UNDERSTANDING GPIO PINS AND FUNCTIONS

Your Raspberry Pi isn't just a tiny computer—it's also a powerful tool for building electronic projects! Thanks to its GPIO (General-Purpose Input/Output) pins, you can connect and control things like LEDs, sensors, and motors. This makes the Raspberry Pi perfect for hobbyists, engineers, and anyone interested in electronics or the Internet of Things (IoT).

If you want to go beyond basic computing, understanding how these pins work is essential. This guide will help you learn what GPIO pins do, how to use them, and how to safely connect components to bring your projects to life.

What Are GPIO Pins?

GPIO pins are the physical connectors on your Raspberry Pi that let it send and receive signals from external devices. You can program them to:

- **Read data (Input):** Detect signals from sensors or buttons.
- **Send signals (Output):** Control LEDs, motors, and other components.

Key Features of GPIO Pins:

- **Input & Output Flexibility**: Each pin can either read signals or send them.
- **Digital Signals:** Pins work with two states—HIGH (3.3V) or LOW (0V)—like a simple on/off switch.
- **More Than Just Basics**: GPIO pins support advanced communication like PWM (for dimming LEDs or controlling motors), I2C, SPI, and UART for connecting to other devices.

The Raspberry Pi GPIO Layout

Most Raspberry Pi models, like the Pi 4, Pi 3, and Pi Zero, have a 40-pin header, though older versions may have fewer. These pins serve different purposes:

- GPIO Pins: Used for general input and output tasks.
- Power Pins: Provide 3.3V or 5V power to external components.
- Ground (GND) Pins: Essential for completing electrical circuits.
- Special Function Pins: Support I2C, SPI, and UART communication.

Understanding GPIO Pin Numbering

There are two common ways to reference GPIO pins when programming:

1. Physical Pin Numbering: Based on their actual location (e.g., Pin 1, Pin 2).

2. BCM (Broadcom) Numbering: Uses the internal system of the Raspberry Pi's processor (e.g., GPIO 17, GPIO 18). This is the preferred method for Python programming.

Types of GPIO Pins and Their Functions

Not all pins are the same! Here's a quick breakdown:

1. Power Pins (3.3V and 5V)

3.3V Pins: Provide steady 3.3V power, which is ideal for most sensors and components.

5V Pins: Used for devices that require more power. However, connecting 5V directly to a GPIO pin can damage your Raspberry Pi, so be careful!

2. Ground Pins (GND)

These pins act as the return path for electrical circuits. You'll need them when connecting components like LEDs and sensors.

3. GPIO Pins (General Purpose)

These are the most commonly used pins, allowing you to:

- Read data from sensors.
- Turn devices on and off (e.g., controlling LEDs or motors).

4. Special Function Pins

Some pins have extra capabilities:

- I2C: Uses SDA and SCL pins to connect multiple devices with just two wires.
- SPI: Supports fast data transfer for devices like touchscreens and SD cards.
- UART: Enables serial communication, commonly used for debugging or connecting to microcontrollers.

Safety Tips for Using GPIO Pins

To keep your Raspberry Pi and components safe, follow these key precautions:

1. Watch the Voltage

GPIO pins work at 3.3V, and connecting anything higher (like 5V) without a voltage converter can fry your board.

2. Use Resistors to Limit Current

When connecting LEDs or motors, always use a resistor to prevent too much current from damaging your Raspberry Pi or components.

3. Double-Check Your Wiring

Before turning your Raspberry Pi on, check your connections carefully to avoid short circuits, which could permanently damage the board.

4. Turn Off Before Changing Connections

To prevent electrical mishaps, power down your Raspberry Pi before plugging or unplugging wires.

Getting Started: Controlling Raspberry Pi's GPIO Pins with Python

Python is one of the easiest and most popular ways to control GPIO pins on a Raspberry Pi, thanks to its simple syntax and built-in support through libraries like RPi.GPIO. If you're new to this, don't worry! This guide will walk you through the basics of setting up and programming GPIO pins using Python.

Step 1: Preparing Your Raspberry Pi

Before jumping into coding, make sure your Raspberry Pi OS is installed and ready. Python and the RPi.GPIO library usually come pre-installed, but it's a good idea to update your system to ensure everything is working smoothly.

Updating Your Raspberry Pi

To keep your system up to date, open the Terminal and enter the following commands:

```bash
sudo apt update

sudo apt upgrade -y
```

Then, verify that the RPi.GPIO library is installed (it should be by default):

```bash
sudo apt install python3-rpi.gpio
```

With your system updated and the required tools in place, you're ready to start working with GPIO pins!

Step 2: Setting Up GPIO Pins in Python

To get started, let's create a simple project that turns an LED on and off using GPIO pin 17. This will help you understand the basics of setting up and controlling GPIO pins with Python.

Wiring the Circuit

Follow these steps to connect an LED to your Raspberry Pi:

- Use GPIO pin 17 (following the BCM numbering system).
- Place a 330-ohm resistor in series with the LED to prevent excess current from damaging it.
- Connect the long leg (anode) of the LED to GPIO 17.
- Connect the short leg (cathode) to the resistor, and then to GND (ground).

Once everything is wired up, you're all set to write Python code to control the LED!

Python Code to Blink an LED:

```python
import RPi.GPIO as GPIO
import time

# Set up GPIO using BCM numbering
GPIO.setmode(GPIO.BCM)

# Set up GPIO pin 17 as an output
GPIO.setup(17, GPIO.OUT)

try:
    while True:
        GPIO.output(17, GPIO.HIGH)   # Turn on the LED
        time.sleep(1)                # Wait for one second
        GPIO.output(17, GPIO.LOW)    # Turn off the LED
        time.sleep(1)                # Wait for one second
except KeyboardInterrupt:
    GPIO.cleanup()  # Clean up GPIO settings on exit
```

Let's break down the key commands used to control GPIO pins on a Raspberry Pi with Python:

- `GPIO.setmode(GPIO.BCM)` – This tells the Raspberry Pi to use the BCM numbering system, which assigns numbers based on the Broadcom chip instead of the physical pin layout.

- `GPIO.setup(17, GPIO.OUT)` – Sets GPIO pin 17 as an output, allowing it to send signals to devices like LEDs.

- `GPIO.output(17, GPIO.HIGH)` – Turns the LED on by sending a 3.3V (HIGH signal) through GPIO 17.

- `GPIO.cleanup()` – Cleans up the GPIO settings when the script stops, preventing potential errors when running another program later.

Using GPIO Pins to Receive Input

GPIO pins aren't just for sending signals—they can also read data from buttons, sensors, and other components. Let's look at an example where pressing a button will turn an LED on or off.

Connecting the Button and LED

- Attach a push button between GPIO pin 18 and GND (ground).

- Use a 10k-ohm pull-up resistor between GPIO 18 and 3.3V to ensure the button functions properly.

- Keep the LED circuit the same, connected to GPIO pin 17.

With this setup, you can write a Python script to detect when the button is pressed and control the LED accordingly.

Python Code to Read Button Input:

```
import RPi.GPIO as GPIO
import time

# Set up GPIO using BCM numbering
GPIO.setmode(GPIO.BCM)

# Set up GPIO pins
GPIO.setup(17, GPIO.OUT)  # LED
GPIO.setup(18, GPIO.IN, pull_up_down=GPIO.PUD_UP)  # Button with pull-up resistor

try:
    while True:
        button_state = GPIO.input(18)  # Read the button state
        if button_state == GPIO.LOW:   # Button pressed
            GPIO.output(17, GPIO.HIGH) # Turn on the LED
        else:
            GPIO.output(17, GPIO.LOW)  # Turn off the LED
        time.sleep(0.1)  # Short delay to debounce the button
except KeyboardInterrupt:
    GPIO.cleanup()  # Clean up GPIO settings on exit
```

Code Explanation:

Setting Up the Button Input – The command `GPIO.setup(18, GPIO.IN, pull_up_down=GPIO.PUD_UP)` configures GPIO pin 18 as an input and enables a built-in pull-up resistor. This helps keep the signal steady when the button isn't pressed.

How It Works – The program monitors the button's state and controls the LED accordingly—turning it on when the button is pressed and off when it's released.

Why This Matters – This basic concept is key for making interactive projects, like triggering actions based on user input or sensor data.

Advancing Your GPIO Skills

Now that you're comfortable with basic input and output, let's move on to more advanced projects. These will introduce Pulse Width Modulation (PWM), analog input using an ADC (Analog-to-Digital Converter), and sensor communication via I2C and SPI.

Project: Adjusting LED Brightness with PWM

PWM (Pulse Width Modulation) is a way to control devices—like LEDs and motors—by rapidly switching them on and off instead of just keeping them fully on or off. This allows you to adjust brightness or speed smoothly.

Key PWM Concepts

Duty Cycle: This determines how long the signal stays on during each cycle. For example, if the LED is on 50% of the time, it appears half as bright.

Frequency: This is how fast the signal turns on and off per second (measured in Hertz (Hz)). A higher frequency results in smoother, flicker-free control.

Wiring the LED for PWM Control

1. Connect an LED to GPIO pin 18 (BCM numbering).

2. Use a 330-ohm resistor in series to prevent damage to the LED.

3. Attach the long leg (anode) of the LED to GPIO pin 18.

4. Connect the short leg (cathode) to the resistor, then to GND (ground).

With this setup, you can use a Python script to adjust the LED's brightness, giving you precise control over its glow.

Python Code for PWM Control:

```python
import RPi.GPIO as GPIO
import time

# Set up GPIO using BCM numbering
GPIO.setmode(GPIO.BCM)

# Set up GPIO pin 18 as an output and initialize PWM
GPIO.setup(18, GPIO.OUT)
pwm_led = GPIO.PWM(18, 1000)  # Set PWM on pin 18 at 1kHz frequency
pwm_led.start(0)  # Start PWM with 0% duty cycle (off)

try:
    while True:
        # Gradually increase brightness
        for duty_cycle in range(0, 101, 5):  # 0% to 100% duty cycle
            pwm_led.ChangeDutyCycle(duty_cycle)
            time.sleep(0.1)
        # Gradually decrease brightness
        for duty_cycle in range(100, -1, -5):  # 100% to 0% duty cycle
            pwm_led.ChangeDutyCycle(duty_cycle)
            time.sleep(0.1)
except KeyboardInterrupt:
    pwm_led.stop()  # Stop the PWM signal
    GPIO.cleanup()  # Clean up GPIO settings on exit
```

Understanding the Code

Starting PWM on GPIO Pin 18 – The command `GPIO.PWM(18, 1000)` activates Pulse Width Modulation (PWM) on GPIO pin 18, setting the signal frequency to 1,000 Hz (1 kHz).

Adjusting LED Brightness – Using `pwm_led.ChangeDutyCycle(duty_cycle)`, we can control how long the LED stays on during each cycle, making it brighter or dimmer.

Creating a Smooth Fading Effect – The script gradually increases and decreases brightness, giving the LED a soft breathing effect.

Where PWM is Useful

Motor Speed Control – Adjust the speed of DC motors or control servo motor positions.

Dimming LED Lights – Use it for adjustable lighting in smart home setups.

Generating Sounds – PWM can also create different tones when driving small speakers.

Reading Analog Sensors with an ADC (Analog-to-Digital Converter)

Since the Raspberry Pi's GPIO pins only recognize digital signals (ON or OFF), you need an ADC chip to read analog signals from sensors like temperature sensors, light sensors, or potentiometers. The MCP3008 ADC chip is a great option for this.

Setting Up the MCP3008 with Raspberry Pi

What You'll Need:

- MCP3008 ADC chip
- An analog sensor (such as a light sensor or potentiometer)
- Breadboard and jumper wires

How to Connect the MCP3008

1. Power the MCP3008

- VDD and VREF → Connect to 3.3V
- AGND and DGND → Connect to GND

2. Connect SPI Communication Pins:

- CLK (Clock) → GPIO 11
- DOUT (Data Out / MISO) → GPIO 9
- DIN (Data In / MOSI) → GPIO 10
- CS (Chip Select) → GPIO 8

3. Hook Up Your Analog Sensor

Attach the sensor's output (e.g., a potentiometer's middle pin) to Channel 0 (CH0) on the MCP3008.

Once set up, your Raspberry Pi can now read analog sensor values, enabling you to create projects like light-sensitive automation, temperature-based triggers, or interactive controls.

CONNECTING SENSORS AND MODULES

Welcome to the world of Raspberry Pi sensors and actuators! If you're eager to bring your DIY projects to life, you're in the right place. Whether you're a complete beginner or a seasoned maker, this guide will walk you through the essentials, introduce you to cool projects, and help troubleshoot common issues. So, grab your Raspberry Pi, and let's jump in!

What Are Sensors and Actuators?

Before we dive in, let's break down these key components:

Sensors – These detect changes in the environment, such as temperature, light, or motion, and convert them into signals that the Raspberry Pi can read.

Actuators – These take signals from the Raspberry Pi and perform actions, like turning on a motor, adjusting brightness, or moving an object.

Think of sensors as the "eyes and ears" of your project and actuators as the "hands and feet." Together, they allow your Raspberry Pi to interact with the physical world.

Why Use Raspberry Pi for Sensors and Actuators?

ou might wonder why Raspberry Pi is a great choice when microcontrollers like Arduino can also handle sensors and actuators. Here's why the Raspberry Pi stands out:

☑ Runs a Full Operating System – Supports multiple programming languages and tools.

☑ Built-in Wi-Fi & Bluetooth – Makes it easy to connect devices and send data.

☑ More Processing Power – Can handle advanced tasks like image recognition and machine learning.

While Arduino is great for simple tasks, the Raspberry Pi is better suited for projects that need more computing power and internet connectivity.

Setting Up Your Raspberry Pi

Before working with sensors and actuators, you'll need to set up your Raspberry Pi. Here's what you need:

- A Raspberry Pi board (Pi 4 or Pi 5 recommended)
- A microSD card with Raspberry Pi OS installed
- A power supply
- A monitor, keyboard, and mouse (or set up remote access)

Steps to Get Started:

1. Insert the microSD card into your Raspberry Pi.

2. Connect a monitor, keyboard, and mouse.

3. Plug in the power supply.

4. Follow the on-screen setup instructions for Raspberry Pi OS.

If you're new to Raspberry Pi, the official Raspberry Pi website offers step-by-step guides to help you get started.

Connecting a Sensor to Your Raspberry Pi

Now that your Raspberry Pi is ready, let's connect a sensor to start gathering real-world data. We'll use a DHT11 temperature and humidity sensor, which is inexpensive and easy to use.

What You'll Need:

- DHT11 Sensor
- Breadboard & Jumper Wires
- 10kΩ Resistor (to stabilize the data signal)

How to Wire It Up:

1. Power (VCC) → Connect to a 3.3V pin on your Raspberry Pi.

2. Ground (GND) → Connect to a GND pin on your Raspberry Pi.

3. Data Signal (DATA) → Connect to GPIO4 on your Raspberry Pi.

4. Resistor Setup → Attach one end of the 10kΩ resistor to the DATA pin and the other to the 3.3V pin.

Once everything is connected, your Raspberry Pi will be able to read temperature and humidity from the sensor. From here, you can write a simple Python script to display the readings and even set up alerts based on the data!

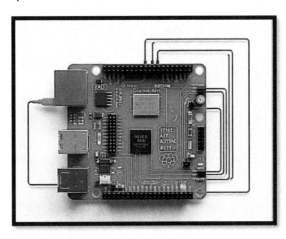

Reading Data from Your Sensor

Now that everything is set up, let's start gathering temperature and humidity data using Python, the most common language for Raspberry Pi projects.

Step 1: Install the Necessary Library

Before we can read sensor data, we need to install the Adafruit_DHT library. Open the terminal on your Raspberry Pi and type:

```bash
sudo apt-get update
sudo apt-get install python3-dev python3-pip
sudo python3 -m pip install --upgrade pip
sudo python3 -m pip install Adafruit_DHT
```

This ensures your Raspberry Pi has everything needed to communicate with the DHT11 sensor.

Step 2: Write a Python Script to Read Sensor Data

Next, we'll create a simple program to collect temperature and humidity readings. You can use a text editor like nano or Thonny (which comes pre-installed with Raspberry Pi OS).

Open a new Python file and enter the following code:

```python
import Adafruit_DHT

import time

sensor = Adafruit_DHT.DHT11  # Defines the sensor type

pin = 4  # Connects the sensor to GPIO pin 4

while True:

    humidity, temperature = Adafruit_DHT.read_retry(sensor, pin)


    if humidity is not None and temperature is not None:

    print (f'Temperature: {temperature:.1f}°C  Humidity: {humidity:.1f}%')

    else:

        print('Error reading sensor data. Retrying...')

    time.sleep(2)  # Waits 2 seconds before taking another reading
```

Step 3: Run Your Script

Save the file and execute it with:

```bash
python3 your_script_name.py
```

If everything is connected properly, you'll see temperature and humidity readings displayed in the terminal every two seconds. If the reading fails, the script will automatically try again.

BUILDING SIMPLE ELECTRONIC CIRCUITS

The Raspberry Pi 5 is a fantastic tool for learning electronics and creating interactive projects. Whether you're a beginner or an experienced maker, you can easily build simple circuits using components like LEDs, buttons, and sensors. Let's dive in and explore some fun projects!

What You'll Need

Before you start, gather these essential items:

- Raspberry Pi 5 with Raspberry Pi OS installed
- Breadboard for easy circuit assembly
- Jumper wires to connect components
- Resistors (330Ω works well for LEDs)
- LEDs to visualize output signals
- Push button to control input
- Optional sensors (e.g., temperature, motion)

Project 1: Making an LED Blink

Step 1: Connect the LED

1. Insert the LED into the breadboard.

2. Connect a 330Ω resistor between the LED's shorter leg (cathode) and GND (ground) on the Raspberry Pi.

3. Connect the LED's longer leg (anode) to GPIO 18 on the Raspberry Pi.

Step 2: Write a Simple Python Script

Now, let's create a Python script to make the LED blink:

```python
import RPi.GPIO as GPIO
import time
# Set up GPIO
```

```
GPIO.setmode(GPIO.BCM)

GPIO.setup(18, GPIO.OUT)  # Set GPIO 18 as an output

try:

    while True:

        GPIO.output(18, GPIO.HIGH)  # Turn LED on

        time.sleep(1)  # Wait 1 second

        GPIO.output(18, GPIO.LOW)  # Turn LED off

        time.sleep(1)  # Wait 1 second

except KeyboardInterrupt:

    GPIO.cleanup()  # Reset GPIO settings when script stops
```

Step 3: Run the Script

1. Save your script as led_blink.py.

2. Open the terminal and run:

   ```bash
   python3 led_blink.py
   ```

Your LED should now blink on and off every second!

Project 2: Turning an LED On and Off with a Button

Let's take it a step further and control the LED using a push button.

Step 1: Connect the Button

1. Connect one leg of the button to GPIO 23.

2. Connect the other leg to GND.

3. Keep your LED setup from the previous project.

Step 2: Write the Code

```python
```

```python
import RPi.GPIO as GPIO
import time
# Set up GPIO
GPIO.setmode(GPIO.BCM)
GPIO.setup(18, GPIO.OUT)  # LED as output
GPIO.setup(23, GPIO.IN, pull_up_down=GPIO.PUD_UP)  # Button as input with pull-up resistor
try:
    while True:
        if GPIO.input(23) == GPIO.LOW:  # Button is pressed
            GPIO.output(18, GPIO.HIGH)  # Turn LED on
        else:
            GPIO.output(18, GPIO.LOW)  # Turn LED off
        time.sleep(0.1)  # Small delay to prevent bouncing issues
except KeyboardInterrupt:
    GPIO.cleanup()  # Reset GPIO settings when script stops
```
```

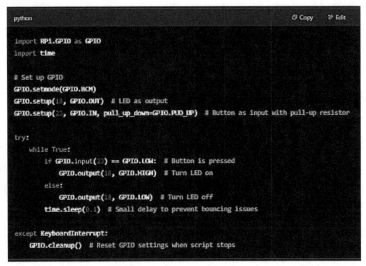
```

Step 3: Run the Script

1. Save your script as button_led.py.

2. In the terminal, run:

```bash
python3 button_led.py
```

Now, pressing the button will turn the LED on!

Where to Go Next?

- Try using multiple LEDs or different colors.

- Experiment with motion or temperature sensors.

- Learn about PWM (Pulse Width Modulation) to control LED brightness.

Want to try something new? Let me know how I can help! 😊

CHAPTER 4

NETWORKING AND REMOTE ACCESS

Getting your Raspberry Pi connected to a network is a key step for most projects. Your Pi has two main network options: a wired connection via Ethernet (eth0) and a wireless connection via WiFi (wlan0).

For a wired setup, just insert an Ethernet cable into your Pi and it will automatically set itself up using DHCP.

To connect via WiFi, you'll need to update the `wpa_supplicant.conf` file with your network details. Your Pi can use either a dynamic IP (assigned automatically by DHCP) or a static IP (manually set). A static IP is helpful for servers or remote access, while DHCP is simpler for most general uses.

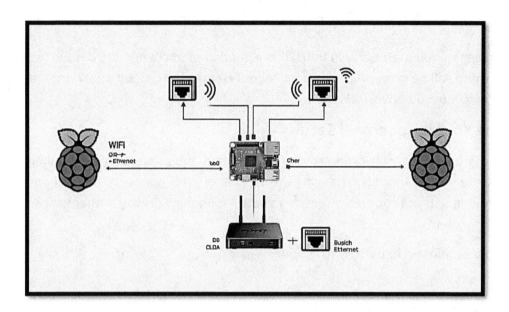

A diagram illustrating how the Raspberry Pi connects to a network, showing both wired (Ethernet) and wireless (WiFi) connections, along with a simple overview of the network structure.

Here are some key network settings to be aware of:

- IP Address (such as 192.168.1.100) – The address of your Pi on the network

- Subnet Mask (usually 255.255.255.0) – Indicates the local area network range

- Default Gateway – The IP address of your router

- DNS Servers (like Google's 8.8.8.8) – Help resolve domain names

To verify your current network settings, type:

```
```

nip addr
```
```

To check if your Pi is online, type:

```
```

ping google.com

114

```
```

If you have multiple Raspberry Pi units, it is a good idea to change the default hostname so that there will be no conflict. Also, for security, reset the default password and disable any unused network services.

Keeping Your Raspberry Pi Secure

Securing your Raspberry Pi protects your information and prevents it from falling into unauthorized hands. Start by changing the default 'pi' user password to a unique and strong one. If you will connect remotely to your Pi, enable SSH key authentication in place of passwords.

Keep your system up to date by executing:

```
```

sudo apt update && sudo apt upgrade

```
```

This ensures that you're running the latest security patches.

As additional security, install a firewall with UFW (Uncomplicated Firewall) by running:

```
```

sudo ufw enable

```
```

Accept network traffic on only those ports your project requires.

If you're using your Pi as a server, consider installing fail2ban, which keeps attempts at logging away from repeating IP addresses, protecting against brute-force attacks.

Other security best practices are:

- Disabling unnecessary services to reduce vulnerabilities
- Creating a separate user account instead of using the default 'pi' user for everyday tasks
- Restricting 'sudo' privileges to minimize risk
- Placing the Pi on a separate VLAN or network segment for better isolation, especially if hosting public services

- Monitoring system logs for any suspicious transactions and setting up alerts for potential security threats

Accessing Your Raspberry Pi Remotely

Enabling and Using SSH

SSH (Secure Shell) enables you to access your Raspberry Pi from a remote machine. To enable SSH:

- If your Pi has a screen, go to Raspberry Pi Configuration, under the Interfaces tab, and enable SSH.

- For a headless setup (no monitor), place an empty file named `ssh` (without an extension) in the boot partition of your SD card before starting the Pi for the first time.

Once SSH is enabled, find your Pi's IP address by running:

```
```

```
hostname -I
```

```
```

Then, from another computer:

- On Linux/macOS, open a terminal and enter:

```
```

```
ssh pi@your_pi_ip_address
```

```
```

- On Windows, use PuTTY or Windows Terminal.

If you connect for the first time, you'll be asked to accept the Pi's SSH fingerprint. The initial login is:

- Username: `pi`

- Password: `raspberry` (set this to a new password at the earliest possible opportunity using `passwd`)

Securing SSH

To add an additional layer of security, set up SSH key authentication instead of using passwords:

1. Generate an SSH key on your machine:

```
ssh-keygen -t rsa -b 4096
```

2. Copy your public key to the Raspberry Pi:

```
ssh-copy-id pi@your_pi_ip_address
```

This provides secure, password-less access to your Pi.

With SSH installed, you can remote-control your Raspberry Pi for purposes of development, debugging, and administration.

The SSH terminal session showing common remote access commands

ACCESSING YOUR RASPBERRY PI REMOTELY WITH VNC

VNC (Virtual Network Computing) lets you control your Raspberry Pi's desktop from another device, making it convenient when you don't have a monitor connected.

How to Enable VNC

1. Update Your System – Before setting up VNC, ensure your Pi is running the latest updates by entering:

```
sudo apt update
sudo apt upgrade
```

2. Turn On VNC – Open the Raspberry Pi Configuration tool from the desktop menu or run:

```
sudo raspi-config
```

Go to "Interface Options" and enable VNC. This will start the VNC server automatically each time your Pi powers on.

3. Connect from Another Device – Install a VNC viewer, such as RealVNC, on your computer. Enter your Pi's IP address in the viewer to establish a connection.

KEEPING YOUR CONNECTION SECURE

- Set a strong password to protect remote access.
- Enable encryption in the VNC server settings.
- If accessing over the internet, set up port forwarding (VNC uses port 5900) and take security precautions.

A strong network connection ensures smoother performance while using VNC remotely.

Managing Your Raspberry Pi Through a Web Interface

Several web-based tools allow you to manage your Raspberry Pi easily through a browser.

Handy Web Management Tools

- **Webmin** – A powerful browser-based dashboard for managing system settings, users, and network configurations. Access it via your Pi's IP address on port 10000.

- **Cockpit** – A sleek, lightweight tool for monitoring system resources and managing services in real-time.

- **Pi-hole** – If using your Pi as an ad-blocker, Pi-hole's dashboard lets you monitor network activity and manage blocklists.

- **Raspberry Pi Web Interface** – A beginner-friendly tool for basic system settings, accessible on port 80.

- **Apache & phpMyAdmin** – Manage web hosting and databases through an easy-to-use web interface.

Security Measures to Follow

o Use strong passwords to protect your web interfaces.

o Enable SSL encryption for secure access.

Turning Your Raspberry Pi into a Home Server

A Raspberry Pi can function as a compact, energy-efficient home server for various tasks.

Getting Started

1. Install a lightweight server OS like Raspberry Pi OS Lite or Ubuntu Server.

2. Assign a static IP address for consistent access.

3. Choose the right applications for your needs:

- File sharing – Samba or NextCloud

- Media streaming – Plex or Jellyfin

- Web hosting – Apache or Nginx

- Network storage (NAS) – External drives or RAID setup

- Home automation – Manage smart home devices

Optimizing Performance and Security

- Use a UPS (Uninterruptible Power Supply) to prevent data loss during power outages.

- Enable SSH key-based authentication for secure remote access.

- Set up a firewall (UFW) to protect your server from unauthorized access.
- Schedule automatic backups and regular system updates.

If you want to manage multiple services easily, consider using Docker containers to keep your setup organized.

Monitoring Your Network with Raspberry Pi

Your Raspberry Pi can serve as a dedicated network monitoring tool to track system performance and network activity.

Essential Monitoring Tools

- Nagios – Monitors system health and service availability. Install with:

```
sudo apt-get install nagios3
```

Wireshark – Analyzes network traffic and helps troubleshoot issues. Install with:

```
sudo apt-get install wireshark
```

Cacti – Provides visual graphs of network activity over time. Install with:

```
sudo apt-get install cacti
```

ntop – Shows real-time network usage in a simple web interface. Install with:

```
sudo apt-get install ntop
```

Zabbix – A powerful tool for monitoring multiple network devices and services with advanced alerts.

Since some of these tools require a lot of processing power, it's best to run only the ones you need and adjust monitoring intervals for better performance.

By setting up these tools, you can easily manage your Raspberry Pi and network from anywhere while keeping everything secure.

Dashboard interface showing network monitoring statistics and graphs

Setting Up a Remote Development Environment on Raspberry Pi

A remote development setup on your Raspberry Pi allows you to code and manage projects efficiently, even when you're not physically near the device.

Getting Started with Remote Access

To work on your Raspberry Pi from another computer, you'll first need to enable SSH (Secure Shell), which lets you connect securely over a network. You can activate SSH in one of two ways:

- Open the Raspberry Pi Configuration tool and turn on SSH.
- Create a blank file named 'ssh' in the boot folder of your Pi's SD card.

Installing Development Tools

Once SSH is enabled, install tools that make coding easier, such as:

- **Visual Studio Code** – A powerful code editor with remote development support.
- **Python IDLE** – A simple interface for writing and testing Python code.
- **Vim** – A lightweight text editor for coding in the terminal.

These tools help with writing, debugging, and managing code on your Raspberry Pi.

Improving Workflow and Performance

To make development smoother, set up Git for version control and configure your favorite IDE (Integrated Development Environment) to support remote development. Many modern IDEs have extensions that allow you to work on your Raspberry Pi as if it were running on your main computer.

For better performance, you can also use cross-compilation—this means writing and compiling code on a more powerful computer and then running it on the Raspberry Pi.

Security and Backups

- Use SSH keys instead of passwords for safer authentication.

- Adjust firewall settings to protect your Pi from unauthorized access.

- Regularly back up your work to avoid losing important files if the SD card fails.

Exploring the Networking Capabilities of Raspberry Pi

The Raspberry Pi is a versatile tool for networking, offering possibilities for both beginners and advanced users. You can use it for a home media server, ad blocker, IoT project, or network monitoring system.

Building a Strong Foundation

Start with the basics:

- Ensure a stable network connection by configuring your Pi properly.

- Learn basic networking concepts so you can troubleshoot issues.

- Gradually expand your projects, adding more complexity as you gain confidence.

Next Steps and Advanced Projects

If you're new to networking on Raspberry Pi, try simple projects like:

- Setting up SSH access for remote control.

- Creating a basic file-sharing server to store and share documents.

Once you're comfortable, take on more advanced projects, such as:

- Setting up a VPN server for secure remote access.
- Building a network monitoring system to track network activity and performance.

Learning and Growing with the Raspberry Pi Community

The Raspberry Pi community offers plenty of resources, tutorials, and forums where you can ask questions and share your experiences. Experimenting with different setups is the best way to learn and develop your skills.

SETTING UP WI-FI AND ETHERNET

If you want to access your Raspberry Pi remotely without worrying about its IP address changing, setting up a static IP is a great solution. This ensures that your Pi always has the same address, making it easier to connect.

This guide is designed for Windows users or those unfamiliar with Linux. It has been updated to reflect the latest Raspbian PIXEL changes, where network settings are now configured in the dhcpcd.conf file instead of the older interfaces file.

What You'll Need:

- A Raspberry Pi
- A network switch (if connecting multiple devices)
- Ethernet cables

Optional:

A Wi-Pi WiFi USB dongle (if you also need wireless connectivity)

Step 1: Check Your Network Settings

Before assigning a static IP, it's a good idea to review your current network setup. This will help you choose the right IP address and avoid conflicts with other devices on the network.

```
pi@raspberrypi: ~                          _ □ ×
File  Edit  Tabs  Help
pi@raspberrypi:~ $ ifconfig
eth0      Link encap:Ethernet  HWaddr b8:27:eb:ef:ef:6b
          inet addr:192.168.1.193  Bcast:192.168.1.255  Mask:255.255.255.0
          inet6 addr: 2602:306:cea8:a320::11/128 Scope:Global
          inet6 addr: fe80::b3ef:fd21:5b73:cd58/64 Scope:Link
          inet6 addr: 2602:306:cea8:a320:e755:76ec:762:96e0/64 Scope:Global
          UP BROADCAST RUNNING MULTICAST  MTU:1500  Metric:1
          RX packets:705 errors:0 dropped:0 overruns:0 frame:0
          TX packets:314 errors:0 dropped:0 overruns:0 carrier:0
          collisions:0 txqueuelen:1000
          RX bytes:42076 (41.0 KiB)  TX bytes:26300 (25.6 KiB)

lo        Link encap:Local Loopback
          inet addr:127.0.0.1  Mask:255.0.0.0
          inet6 addr: ::1/128 Scope:Host
          UP LOOPBACK RUNNING  MTU:65536  Metric:1
          RX packets:427 errors:0 dropped:0 overruns:0 frame:0
          TX packets:427 errors:0 dropped:0 overruns:0 carrier:0
          collisions:0 txqueuelen:1
          RX bytes:39088 (38.1 KiB)  TX bytes:39088 (38.1 KiB)

pi@raspberrypi:~ $
```

Before making any changes, it's helpful to check your Raspberry Pi's current network configuration.

1. Open LXTerminal or the command prompt on your Raspberry Pi.

2. Type the following command and press Enter:

```
ifconfig
```

3. This will show details about your network connection, including your IP address and other relevant settings.

Backing Up Your Network Configuration

Before making adjustments, it's a good practice to create a backup of your current network settings. This way, you can restore them if anything goes wrong.

```
pi@raspberrypi: ~                          _ □ ×
File  Edit  Tabs  Help
pi@raspberrypi:~ $ sudo cp /etc/dhcpcd.conf /etc/dhcdcp.backup
pi@raspberrypi:~ $
```

If you're not familiar with Linux, it's a good idea to back up the `dhcpcd.conf` file before making any changes. This way, you can easily restore the original settings if something goes wrong.

To create a backup, open the terminal and run:

```

sudo cp /etc/dhcpcd.conf /etc/dhcpcd.backup

```

This makes a copy of the current configuration so you can roll back any changes if needed.

Step 3: Editing Network Settings

Once you've saved a backup, you can proceed with updating your network configuration.

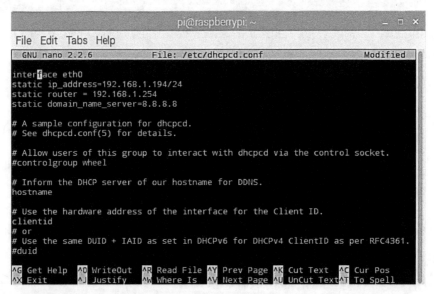

To assign a static IP address to your Raspberry Pi, you'll need to update its network settings. This ensures that your Pi always has the same IP address, making remote access more convenient.

Steps to Modify Network Settings

1. Open the terminal and enter this command to edit the network configuration file:

```
```

sudo nano /etc/dhcpcd.conf

```

2. At the beginning of the file, add these lines to set up a static IP address for the Ethernet connection (`eth0`):

```

interface eth0

static ip_address=10.11.44.124/24

static routers=10.11.44.1

static domain_name_servers=172.16.33.85

```

static ip_address: Change this to the IP address you want your Raspberry Pi to use.

**static routers**: Set this to your network's gateway (usually your router's IP address).

**static domain_name_servers**: If you have a preferred DNS server, enter its address here.

**3. Save and close the file:**

- Press `CTRL + X` to exit the editor.
- Press `Y` to confirm the changes.
- Hit `Enter` to save the file.

## Step 4. Restart Your Raspberry Pi

To apply the changes, restart your Raspberry Pi. After rebooting, it will use the static IP address you assigned.

After making changes to the dhcpcd.conf file, you need to restart your Raspberry Pi for the new network settings to take effect.

**Restarting the Raspberry Pi**
```

To reboot your device, enter the following command in the terminal:

```

sudo reboot

```

This will restart your Raspberry Pi and apply the updated network configuration.

Step 5: Test the New Network Setup

Once the system boots up, confirm that the new static IP address is working correctly.

```
C:\Windows\system32\cmd.exe

Microsoft Windows [Version 6.1.7601]
Copyright (c) 2009 Microsoft Corporation.  All rights reserved.

C:\Users\ajneal>ping 192.168.1.194

Pinging 192.168.1.194 with 32 bytes of data:
Reply from 192.168.1.194: bytes=32 time<1ms TTL=64
Reply from 192.168.1.194: bytes=32 time<1ms TTL=64
Reply from 192.168.1.194: bytes=32 time<1ms TTL=64
Reply from 192.168.1.194: bytes=32 time<1ms TTL=64

Ping statistics for 192.168.1.194:
    Packets: Sent = 4, Received = 4, Lost = 0 (0% loss),
Approximate round trip times in milli-seconds:
    Minimum = 0ms, Maximum = 0ms, Average = 0ms

C:\Users\ajneal>
```

To check if your Raspberry Pi is properly connected to the network, use the ping command. This will help confirm that your Pi can communicate with another device on the same network.

If you're not getting a response, try these troubleshooting steps:

1. Ensure the Ethernet cable is connected – Make sure it's securely plugged into both the Raspberry Pi and the network switch.

2. Double-check your network settings – Verify that the IP address, subnet mask, and gateway are correctly set.

3. Check Windows security settings – If you're trying to ping a Windows computer, keep in mind that some security settings might block ping requests.

USING SSH AND VNC FOR REMOTE CONTROL

The Raspberry Pi is a widely used single-board computer, popular for various applications like smart home automation, robotics, media centers, and even industrial tasks. The latest version, Raspberry Pi 5, launched in October 2023, offers better performance with a more powerful processor, enhanced graphics, and faster memory.

Thanks to its affordability and versatility, the Raspberry Pi is a favorite among hobbyists, educators, and professionals. While it can function as a desktop computer, many users prefer a headless setup, which means running it without a monitor, keyboard, or mouse. This method saves power, reduces extra hardware, and makes remote management easier.

In this guide, we'll go through setting up a headless Raspberry Pi and configuring SSH and VNC to enable remote access and control.

What You'll Need:

- Raspberry Pi 5B/4B (or a compatible model)
- MicroSD card (Class 10, at least 32GB)
- MicroSD card reader
- Power adapter for the Raspberry Pi
- A computer (to set up the MicroSD card)
- Internet connection

Preparing the MicroSD Card

Before setting up your Raspberry Pi, you need to prepare the MicroSD card by installing the necessary software.

1. Insert the MicroSD card into a card reader and connect it to your computer.

2. Format the card to FAT32 using an SD card formatting tool (available for download online).

3. Download and install the Raspberry Pi Imager for your operating system. This tool will help you install the Raspberry Pi operating system onto the MicroSD card.

Once the MicroSD card is ready, you can proceed with installing the OS and enabling remote access to control your Raspberry Pi from another device.

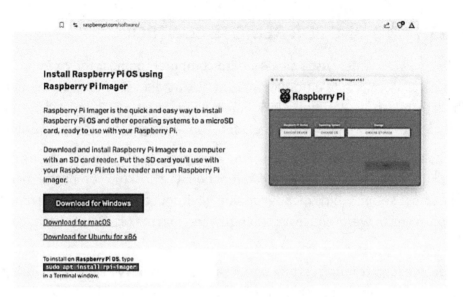

Install and run the Raspberry Pi Imager on your computer.

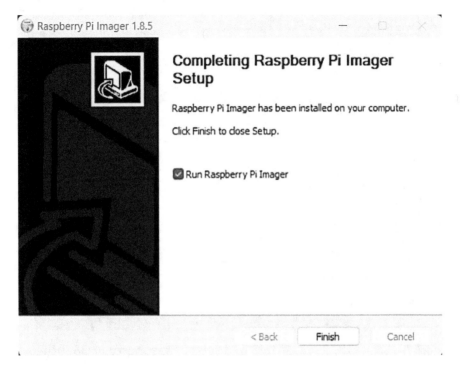

When you open the Raspberry Pi Imager, it appears like this:

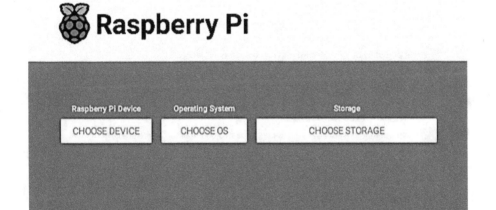

Now, select the "CHOOSE DEVICE" option and pick the Raspberry Pi model you're using. The most recent versions are the Raspberry Pi 5 and Raspberry Pi 4.

For this guide, we'll be setting up the Raspberry Pi 4B.

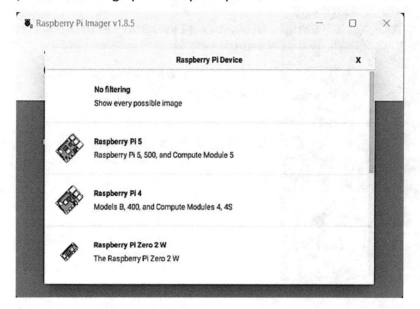

Following, click on the "CHOOSE OS" tab, and select "Raspberry Pi OS (other)."

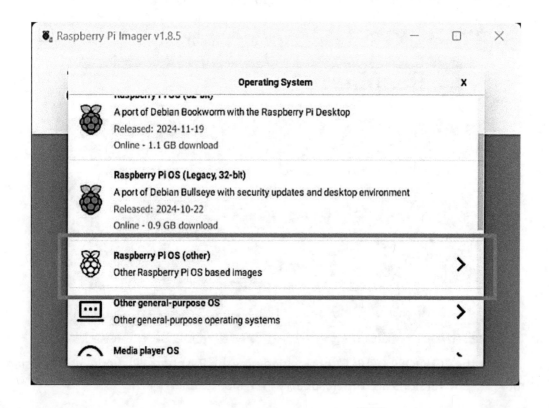

Scroll down and pick "Raspberry Pi OS (Legacy, 64-bit) Full." Alternatively, you can choose another OS version that best suits your requirements.

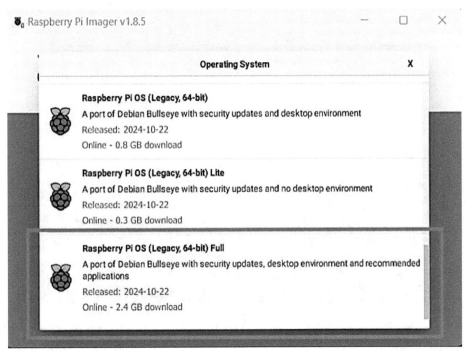

Now, click on "CHOOSE STORAGE" and select the MicroSD card from the list. Ensure the card is properly connected to your computer via an SD card reader.

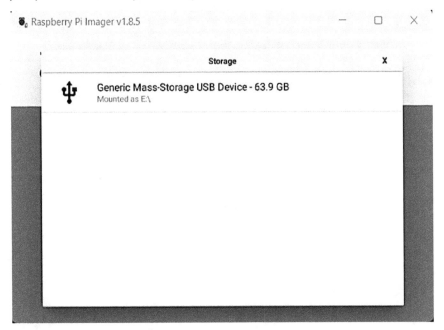

Click "NEXT" to proceed. A pop-up window will appear, asking you to customize the operating system settings. Select "EDIT SETTINGS" to make adjustments.

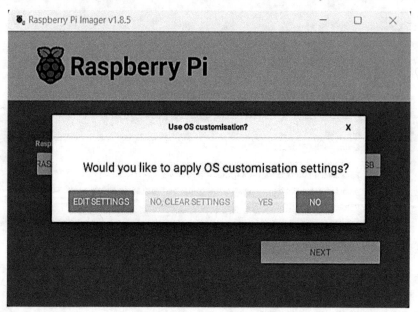

In the General tab, give your Raspberry Pi a name. Then, create a login with a username and password. Connect to Wi-Fi by entering your network name (SSID) and password. Choose your country in the WLAN settings and adjust any regional preferences if necessary.

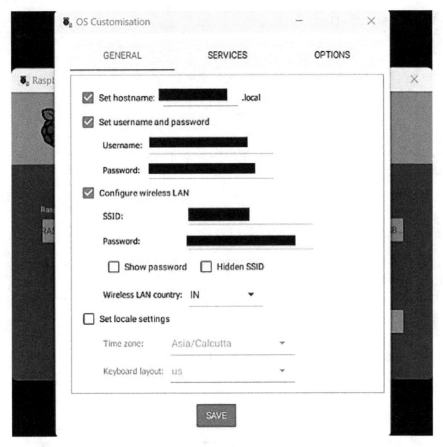

Under the "Services" option', check the "Enable SSH" tab

Click "Yes" to confirm. A message will warn you that all data on the storage device will be deleted. If you're sure you want to proceed, click "Yes" again and allow the setup to continue.

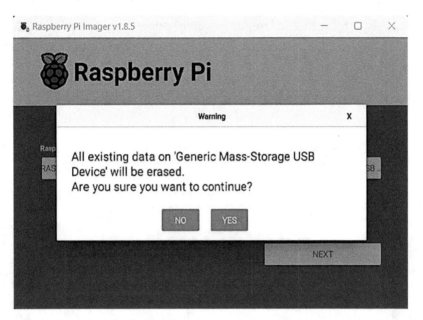

During the setup, files will be copied to your MicroSD card, followed by a verification process to confirm they were written correctly. Although you can choose to skip this step, it's recommended to wait and ensure everything is properly installed.

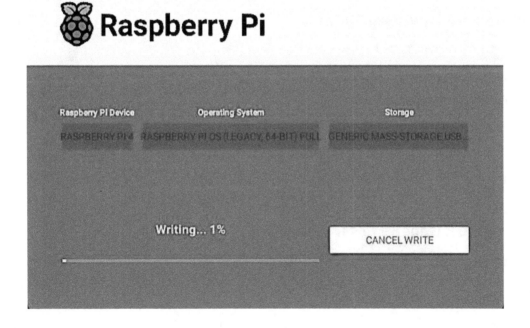

Once the process is complete and the files have been verified, you'll see a message asking you to remove the SD card. Click "Continue" and safely eject the MicroSD card from your computer.

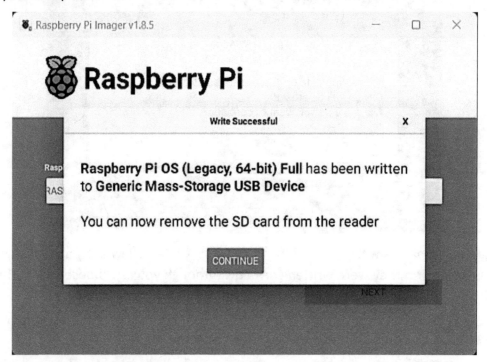

Powering Up Your Raspberry Pi

1. Insert the MicroSD Card

Before turning on the Raspberry Pi, make sure to insert the microSD card that has the operating system installed.

2. Turn on the Raspberry Pi

Plug in the power supply to start the device. You'll see the indicator lights flashing, signaling that the system is booting. Once it's fully powered up, the power LED will stay solid.

Finding the Raspberry Pi's IP Address

To connect to your Raspberry Pi remotely, you need to find its IP address. Since the Wi-Fi details were already set during setup, the Raspberry Pi will automatically connect to your network when powered on.

Here are a few ways to locate the IP address:

- Use a network scanning tool such as Advanced IP Scanner (Windows), Angry IP Scanner, or Zenmap (Nmap).

- Check your router's connected devices list through its admin panel.

- Use your mobile hotspot and look at connected devices.

- If you assigned a hostname during setup, use the ping command in the terminal.

For example, in Windows Command Prompt, type:

```bash
ping pi.local
```

- In this guide, Angry IP Scanner was used to identify the Raspberry Pi's IP address.

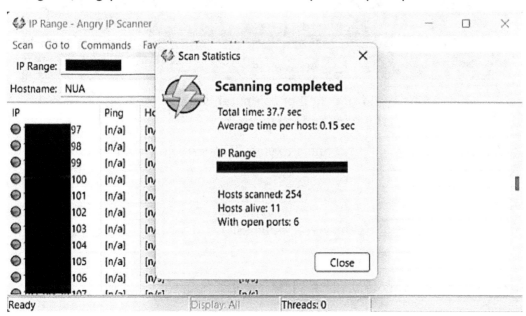

Remotely Accessing Your Raspberry Pi

After identifying your Raspberry Pi's IP address, you can connect to it using an SSH client. SSH (Secure Shell) is a secure way to remotely access and control your Raspberry Pi over a network, making it ideal for headless setups where no monitor, keyboard, or mouse is connected.

If you're using Windows, you can use tools like PuTTY, Bitvise SSH, or MobaXterm. For this guide, we used MobaXterm to establish the connection. You can download it from its official website.

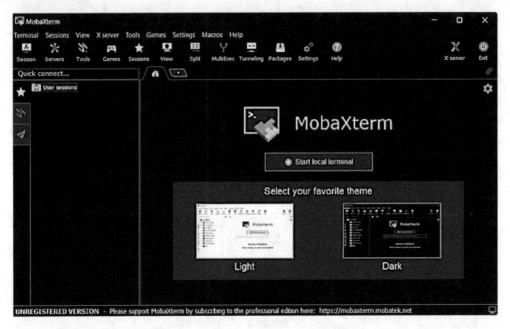

To access your Raspberry Pi from another computer, start by opening a terminal window. Click on "Start local terminal" to launch it.

Next, use the SSH command to connect to your Raspberry Pi. The format for this command is:

```bash
ssh <your-username>@<Raspberry-Pi-IP-address>
```

For example, if your Raspberry Pi's IP address is 192.168.35.02 and your username is pi, type:

```bash
ssh pi@192.168.35.02
```

When prompted, enter the password you set up earlier while preparing the microSD card. If entered correctly, you'll be connected, and you can now control your Raspberry Pi remotely using terminal commands.

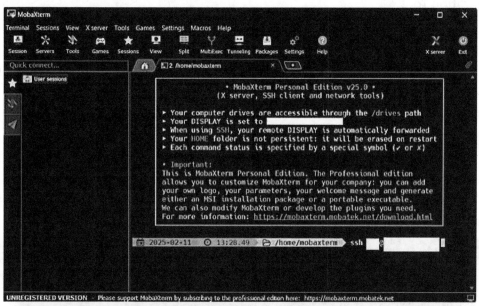

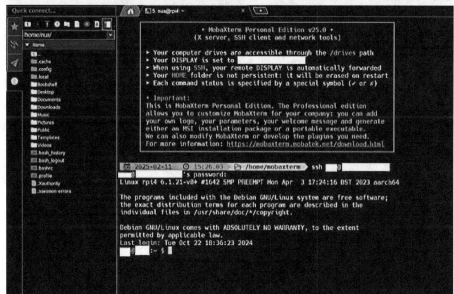

UPDATING RASPBERRY PI'S CONFIGURATION TOOL

After connecting to your Raspberry Pi remotely, the next step is to open and update its Configuration Tool.

1. Launch the SSH tool on your computer and log in to your Raspberry Pi.

2. Once you're logged in, type the following command to access the Raspberry Pi Configuration Tool:

```bash
sudo raspi-config
```

This will open a menu where you can adjust system settings and update your Raspberry Pi as needed.

The Raspberry Pi Configuration Tool will appear in the terminal window of the SSH software you're using (such as MobaXterm in this example). You should see a menu with various system settings that you can modify.

To update the Raspberry Pi Configuration Tool, navigate to the "7. Update" option, press Enter, and the tool will begin updating.

Updating and Upgrading Raspberry Pi Remotely

To ensure your Raspberry Pi is running the latest software, you can update and upgrade it remotely using an SSH client.

1. Connect to your Raspberry Pi via SSH using a tool like MobaXterm.

2. Once logged in, enter the following command in the terminal:

```bash
sudo apt update && sudo apt upgrade -y
```

3. This will check for updates and install any available upgrades automatically. Once finished, your Raspberry Pi will be up to date.

```
        @      :~ $ sudo apt update && sudo apt upgrade -y
        Hit:1 http://security.debian.org/debian-security bullseye-security InRelease
        Hit:2 http://archive.raspberrypi.org/debian bullseye InRelease
        Hit:3 http://deb.debian.org/debian bullseye InRelease
        Hit:4 http://deb.debian.org/debian bullseye-updates InRelease
llow terminal folder    Reading package lists... 90%
```

TURNING ON VNC FOR REMOTE ACCESS

To access your Raspberry Pi's desktop from another device, you need to enable Virtual Network Computing (VNC). VNC lets you use the Raspberry Pi's graphical interface without needing a monitor, keyboard, or mouse directly connected to it.

Unlike SSH, which only provides a command-line interface, VNC gives you full access to the desktop, allowing you to navigate with a mouse, open windows, and use applications as you would on a regular computer.

Setting Up VNC

1. VNC Server on Raspberry Pi

The Raspberry Pi comes with the RealVNC Server pre-installed, so no additional setup is needed on the Pi itself.

2. Install a VNC Viewer on Your Computer

To view and control the Raspberry Pi remotely, install a VNC Viewer on your computer. This will connect to the VNC server running on the Pi and display its desktop.

3. Connect to the Raspberry Pi

Open the VNC Viewer and enter the Raspberry Pi's IP address (along with a display number, if required). Once connected, your Raspberry Pi's desktop will appear on your computer screen, allowing you to control it as if you were using it directly.

Enabling VNC on Raspberry Pi

Before using VNC, you need to enable it:

1. Log in via SSH

   Use an SSH client like MobaXterm to connect to your Raspberry Pi.

2. Open the Configuration Tool

   In the terminal, enter the following command:

   ```bash
   sudo raspi-config
   ```

3. Turn on VNC

   In the Configuration Tool, go to "3. Interface Options" and select it to enable VNC.

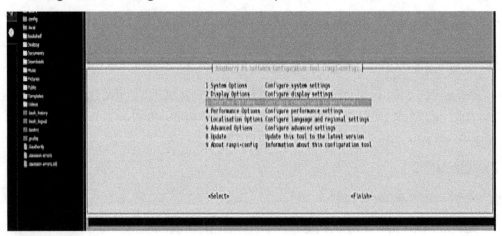

Next, select "I3 VNC."

Then, select "Yes," and press enter to enable the VNC server.

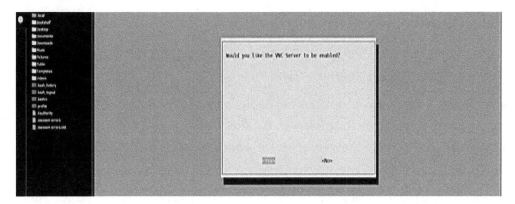

With the VNC server activated, there's one final step to optimize the display. You'll need to adjust the screen resolution to ensure everything appears correctly.

To do this, open the Raspberry Pi Configuration Tool and choose "2 Display Options."

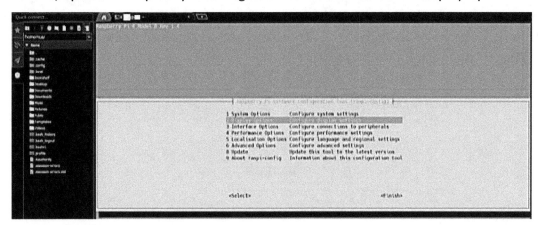

choose the "D5 VNC Resolution."

Select the highest resolution and press, "SELECT."

The resolution will be as selected.

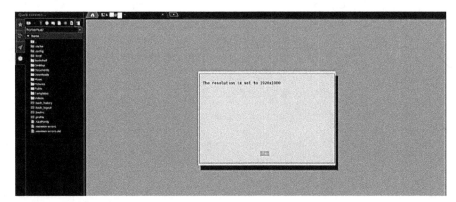

Accessing Raspberry Pi's Desktop Remotely

With VNC enabled on your Raspberry Pi, the next step is to install a VNC Viewer on your computer to access its desktop remotely.

There are various VNC Viewer options available, such as TightVNC Viewer, RealVNC Viewer, and Remmina. Since Raspberry Pi already comes with RealVNC Server pre-installed, we'll use RealVNC Viewer, so there's no need for additional setup on the Raspberry Pi.

Start by downloading and installing RealVNC Viewer on your computer. Open the application and enter your Raspberry Pi's IP address. Press Enter, and a login window will appear, asking for your credentials.

Use the username and password you created during the OS setup (when preparing the SD card). If you want to avoid entering them every time, check the "Remember Password" option. Finally, click "OK" to connect, and you'll see your Raspberry Pi's desktop on your computer screen.

After connecting, you'll be able to control and navigate your Raspberry Pi's desktop right from your computer.

Setting Up the RealVNC Server to Start Automatically

To avoid manually enabling the VNC server each time you want to access your Raspberry Pi remotely, you need to configure it to run automatically at startup.

First, connect to your Raspberry Pi using an SSH client like MobaXterm. Once logged in, enter the following command in the terminal:

```bash
sudo systemctl enable vncserver-x11-serviced
```

This ensures that the VNC server starts automatically whenever your Raspberry Pi is powered on.

To apply the changes right away, restart the VNC server by running:

```bash
sudo systemctl restart vncserver-x11-serviced
```

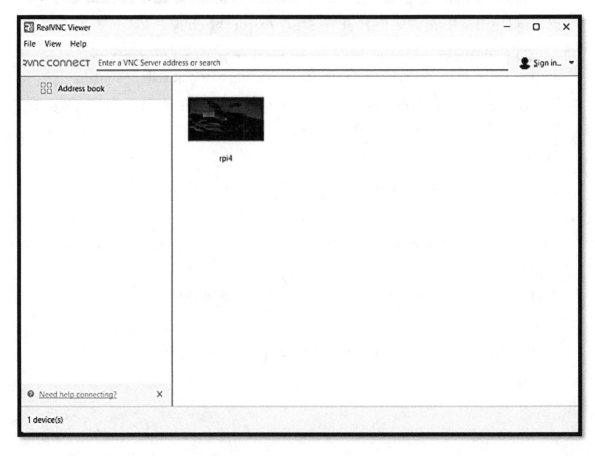

```
 2025-02-11  ⏱ 18:55.12  ▷  /home/mobaxterm  ▷  ssh      @
         @          's password:
Linux rpi4 6.1.21-v8+ #1642 SMP PREEMPT Mon Apr  3 17:24:16 BST 2023 aarch64

The programs included with the Debian GNU/Linux system are free software;
the exact distribution terms for each program are described in the
individual files in /usr/share/doc/*/copyright.

Debian GNU/Linux comes with ABSOLUTELY NO WARRANTY, to the extent
permitted by applicable law.
Last login: Tue Feb 11 18:44:55 2025
    @rpi4:~ $ sudo systemctl enable vncserver-x11-serviced
    @rpi4:~ $ sudo systemctl restart vncserver-x11-serviced
    @rpi4:~ $
```

Now, whenever your Raspberry Pi turns on, the VNC server will start automatically. This allows you to easily connect to its desktop remotely using the VNC Viewer on your computer without any extra setup.

CHAPTER 5

HOME AUTOMATION AND IOT

Raspberry Pi 5: The Future of Home Automation

What once seemed like science fiction—controlling home devices with a tap or voice command—is now an everyday reality. From managing appliances and lighting to enhancing security, smart home automation has become more accessible. However, one major hurdle remains: ensuring that different smart devices work together seamlessly for a hassle-free experience.

That's where the Raspberry Pi 5 comes in. As the most advanced model in the Raspberry Pi series, it delivers the power, reliability, and flexibility needed to serve as the central hub for a smart home. In this guide, we'll explore how the Raspberry Pi 5 can transform your home into an efficient, high-tech space.

The Evolution of Home Automation and Raspberry Pi

To fully understand the impact of the Raspberry Pi 5 on home automation, it's helpful to look at how this technology has developed over time.

Initially, home automation was dominated by expensive, proprietary systems from companies like Crestron and Control4, which were out of reach for most homeowners. Later, more affordable DIY hubs from brands like Nexia, Wink, Vera, and SmartThings became available. However, these solutions often came with drawbacks, such as software limitations, ongoing subscription costs, and limited long-term support.

Everything changed in 2012 with the launch of the first Raspberry Pi—a budget-friendly, Linux-based single-board computer small enough to fit anywhere in a home. Tech enthusiasts quickly recognized its potential for home automation, thanks to its open-source nature and compatibility with add-ons like sensors and relays. With each new version, the Raspberry Pi became more powerful and user-friendly for building customized smart home systems.

Now, with the Raspberry Pi 5, we have a device that offers the processing power, connectivity, and community support necessary to manage a complete home automation setup. Let's take a closer look at what makes it the perfect choice.

WHY THE RASPBERRY PI 5 IS PERFECT FOR HOME AUTOMATION

A smart home hub needs enough computing power and memory to efficiently manage multiple connected devices, automation rules, and user controls. This is where the Raspberry Pi 5 outshines its predecessors and other single-board computers.

With its upgraded hardware and expanded capabilities, the Raspberry Pi 5 is an excellent choice for home automation. Whether you're controlling smart lights, monitoring security cameras, or automating daily routines, this compact yet powerful device ensures that everything operates smoothly and efficiently.

The Raspberry Pi 5 is packed with features that make it an excellent choice for managing a smart home. Here's what makes it stand out:

Quad-core ARM Cortex-A55 CPU up to 2.0GHz

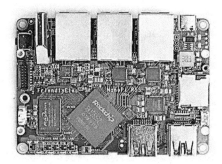

◆NPU: Support 0.8T

◆ 2GB LPDDR4X

◆8GB eMMC

◆GPU: Mali-G52 1-Core-2EE

◆support NVME, PCIe WiFi etc

◆support UHS-I

◆one Native Gigabit Ethernet

◆support 3-D video formats

- **Faster Performance** – With a Rockchip RK3568 Quad-Core ARM Cortex-A55 processor running at 2.4GHz, this model is much more powerful than earlier versions, ensuring smooth operation for automation tasks.

- **More Memory Options – It** comes with 4GB of LPDDR4 RAM as the standard, which is ideal for running Home Assistant, Node-RED, and other automation tools. If you need more or less, there are also 2GB and 8GB models available.

- **Stronger Wireless Connectivity** – Featuring WiFi 6 and Bluetooth 5.0, the Raspberry Pi 5 provides a fast and stable connection for all your smart home devices. WiFi 6 is especially useful for homes with multiple connected gadgets.

- **Reliable Wired Networking –** The Gigabit Ethernet port ensures a stable connection for important devices like security cameras. Plus, with Power over Ethernet (PoE) support, you can power the Raspberry Pi and other connected devices using just one network cable.

- **Plenty of USB Ports** – Equipped with multiple USB 3.0 ports and a USB-C port, you can easily connect sensors, controllers, and other accessories.

- **Supports 4K Video Streaming** – With H.265/HEVC hardware decoding, the Raspberry Pi 5 can handle high-quality 4K video at 60fps, making it a great choice for managing live security camera feeds.

- **Efficient Power Management** – The built-in PoE/PoE+ controller delivers up to 30W of power, which means you can run both the Raspberry Pi 5 and other devices using a single cable, keeping your setup neat and organized.

With improved cooling options, better power regulation, and expandable storage, the Raspberry Pi 5 is designed to be a powerful and reliable hub for home automation, now and in the future.

Best Software Choices for Home Automation on Raspberry Pi 5

Along with its powerful hardware, the Raspberry Pi 5 supports several user-friendly automation platforms. Here are two of the most popular options:

Home Assistant – This is the go-to software for smart home automation, providing an easy-to-use interface, support for a wide range of devices, and advanced automation features. It runs smoothly on the Raspberry Pi 5.

openHAB – A great alternative for users who want maximum customization and control over their smart home setup. While it offers deep automation capabilities, it requires a bit more technical knowledge to configure.

With its combination of high-performance hardware and versatile software, the Raspberry Pi 5 is an affordable and powerful choice for anyone looking to build a custom home automation system.

Home Automation Software Options for Raspberry Pi 5

Aside from Home Assistant and openHAB, the Raspberry Pi 5 supports several other smart home automation platforms:

- Domoticz – A straightforward system that focuses on energy monitoring and device control, offering a simpler interface compared to openHAB.

- Jeedom – A French-language automation system that provides advanced remote management features similar to commercial solutions.

- Node-RED – A visual programming tool that allows you to create custom automation workflows by connecting different smart home devices and services.

All of these options run efficiently on the Raspberry Pi 5, providing easy-to-use dashboards, remote access, and support for a wide range of smart home devices. With active developer communities, these platforms continue to improve, ensuring new features and integrations over time.

Why Raspberry Pi 5 is Better Than Commercial Smart Hubs

You might be wondering why you should build a DIY home automation system with a Raspberry Pi 5 instead of using off-the-shelf hubs like SmartThings or Wink. Here's why the Raspberry Pi 5 is the better option:

Lower Cost – You can build a fully functional home automation system with a Raspberry Pi 5 for under $100, including all necessary accessories. Plus, unlike many commercial hubs, there are no monthly fees.

Total Customization – Open-source software gives you complete control to modify, expand, and customize your system. You're not limited by a company's restrictions— you can add any integration or adjust the interface as needed.

More Reliable – Many commercial hubs rely on cloud servers, meaning if the company has an outage or shuts down, your system could stop working. A Raspberry Pi-based system runs locally, so it stays operational no matter what happens to the manufacturer.

Future-Proof – Commercial hubs often become outdated when manufacturers stop supporting them. With the Raspberry Pi, you can easily upgrade the hardware when a new model comes out while keeping your smart home system intact.

Better Privacy – Unlike commercial hubs that store data on company servers, a Raspberry Pi setup keeps everything on your own network. This means no risk of your data being sold or exposed in security breaches.

The cost savings, customization, reliability, and privacy benefits of a Raspberry Pi smart home setup make it a superior alternative to commercial hubs, even if it requires some initial setup.

Connecting All Your Smart Home Devices

A smart home is more than just turning lights on and off—it involves security, entertainment, climate control, and energy management. The Raspberry Pi 5 is designed to integrate seamlessly with a variety of smart devices, supporting WiFi, Bluetooth, Z-Wave, Zigbee, and IP-based connections. It works with:

- **Smart Home Ecosystems** – Ring, Nest, Philips Hue, SmartThings

- **Security Systems** – Abode, SimpliSafe, Iris

- **Garage & Door Controls** – Chamberlain MyQ, Jeenu, Nexxa

- **Lighting** – Philips Hue, LIFX, TP-Link Kasa

- **Smart Switches & Plugs** – GE, Wemo, Sonoff

- **Thermostats** – ecobee, Honeywell, Tado

- **Security Cameras** – Amcrest, Reolink, Ring

- **Streaming & Media Players** – Chromecast, Apple TV

- **Smart Sensors** – Temperature, motion, water leak, air quality

- Irrigation Systems & Energy Monitors

Because the Raspberry Pi 5 is open-source and highly adaptable, you can also add custom integrations using third-party libraries or programming. This ensures long-term compatibility and future-proofing for your smart home system.

With a Raspberry Pi 5 as your smart home hub, you'll have full control, flexibility, and long-term reliability—all while saving money and keeping your data private.

TURNING YOUR HOME INTO A SMART HOME WITH RASPBERRY PI 5

Now that we've covered how the Raspberry Pi 5 is a powerful and flexible option for home automation, let's go over the steps to set it up and turn your house into a smart home.

1. Choose the Right Hardware

Start with the essentials or expand your setup for more advanced features.

Basic Setup: You'll need a Raspberry Pi 5 board, a case, a power supply, a microSD card, and heatsinks for cooling.

Advanced Setup: Add extras like a wireless keyboard and mouse, touchscreen display, USB hub, cameras, or environmental sensors to enhance functionality.

2. Set Up the Operating System

Install Raspberry Pi OS or a dedicated smart home platform on the microSD card.

Connect your Raspberry Pi to the internet using either WiFi or an Ethernet cable.

3. Install Smart Home Software

Home Assistant is a great choice because it's easy to use and supports many smart devices.

Set up the software to recognize and integrate with the smart gadgets in your home.

4. Expand Your Smart Home Capabilities

Add Zigbee or Z-Wave sticks for compatibility with more smart devices.

Use Node-RED to automate tasks by linking different systems together.

Connect sensors and cameras to monitor your environment or add security features.

5. Automate Your Home

Set up routines to control lights, locks, and thermostats automatically based on time or activity.

Use voice commands with Alexa or Google Assistant for hands-free operation.

Access and manage your smart home remotely from your phone, tablet, or computer.

With this setup, you'll have a smart home that's affordable, customizable, and private—without relying on expensive commercial hubs.

Keeping Your Smart Home Up to Date

One of the best things about Raspberry Pi is that it keeps improving thanks to a strong community of developers. Here's how you can keep your system fresh and future-proof:

- Home Assistant updates frequently, adding new device support and automation options.

- Node-RED expands to integrate even more smart home devices.

- LibreNMS lets you monitor your home network for issues.

- Pi-hole blocks unwanted ads across all devices in your home.

- Security camera setups keep improving, offering better video quality and smart alerts.

- New accessories like touchscreens, smart displays, and gaming emulators add more ways to use your Raspberry Pi.

Because the Raspberry Pi 5 runs open-source software, it will keep evolving, making it a better long-term investment than commercial smart hubs, which often become outdated.

WHY CHOOSE RASPBERRY PI 5 FOR YOUR SMART HOME?

Unlike expensive, closed-system smart home hubs, Raspberry Pi 5 gives you complete control over your home automation. Here's why it stands out:

- **Powerful and Efficient** – Easily handles multiple devices and automation tasks.

- **Budget-Friendly** – No expensive subscription fees or locked-in ecosystems.

- **Fully Customizable** – Set up your smart home exactly how you want it.

- **Secure and Private** – No need to rely on cloud-based services.

If you want a smart home that works on your terms, Raspberry Pi 5 is the way to go. It's affordable, reliable, and flexible enough to adapt as technology evolves.

CONNECTING SMART DEVICES

Take control of your home automation with the Raspberry Pi 5, a powerful and budget-friendly way to manage smart devices. This guide will show you how to set up your Pi as a central hub, install the right software, connect smart devices, and create automation routines—giving you a customized smart home experience without expensive commercial systems.

Why Choose Raspberry Pi 5 for Home Automation?

Many smart home hubs can be costly and restrictive, limiting what you can do with your devices. The Raspberry Pi 5 offers a more affordable and flexible solution, allowing you to build a smart home system that works exactly how you want it.

What Makes Raspberry Pi 5 a Great Choice?

Faster Performance – Its quad-core processor ensures smooth control of multiple smart devices and automation tasks.

Extensive Connectivity – With USB 3.0, GPIO pins, and wireless capabilities, it supports a wide range of smart gadgets and sensors.

Customizable & Cost-Effective – Unlike commercial hubs, the Pi 5 lets you create a system that fits your needs without expensive subscriptions.

With the Raspberry Pi 5, you can build a smart home system that's affordable, powerful, and fully under your control—without being tied to expensive, pre-built solutions.

What You Need to Build a Smart Home Hub

To set up a smart home hub using Raspberry Pi 5, you'll need a few key components:

Raspberry Pi 5 – The main device that powers your smart home system.

MicroSD Card (32GB or more) – Stores the operating system and smart home software.

USB-C Power Supply – Keeps the Raspberry Pi running smoothly.

Smart Devices – Includes smart bulbs, switches, thermostats, and security cameras.

Home Automation Software (Home Assistant) – The platform that helps manage and automate devices.

Additional Sensors & Relays (Optional) – Motion detectors, temperature sensors, and other accessories to expand automation capabilities.

Step 1: Install Raspberry Pi OS & Set Up Home Assistant

Installing Raspberry Pi OS

1. Go to the official Raspberry Pi website and download Raspberry Pi OS.

2. Use Balena Etcher to write the OS onto a microSD card.

3. Insert the card into the Raspberry Pi, connect a monitor and keyboard, and turn it on.

Updating the System

To ensure everything runs smoothly, open the terminal and enter these commands to update the system:

```bash
sudo apt update
sudo apt upgrade
```

Installing Home Assistant

Home Assistant is an easy-to-use software that lets you control and automate your smart home devices. Install it by running:

```bash
```

```
curl -Lo installer.sh https://raw.githubusercontent.com/home-assistant/supervised-
installer/main/installer.sh

sudo bash installer.sh

```
```

Accessing Home Assistant

Once installed, open a web browser and visit:

http://homeassistant.local:8123

Follow the setup instructions to create an account and configure your system. Now, you're ready to start connecting and managing your smart home devices!

```

Step 2: Connecting and Setting Up Smart Devices

With Home Assistant, you can easily connect and manage different smart devices like lights, thermostats, and cameras.

Adding Smart Devices

1. Open Home Assistant and navigate to Settings > Devices & Services.

2. Click Add Integration and select the brand of your smart device (e.g., Philips Hue lights, Nest thermostats).

3. Follow the setup instructions—some devices may need pairing or an API key to connect properly.

Organizing Devices by Room

For better control, group your devices by room:

Go to Configuration > Areas and assign each device to the appropriate space in your home.

This makes managing and automating them more convenient.

TESTING YOUR DEVICES

Once everything is set up, make sure your devices work as expected:

- Try turning them on or off through the Home Assistant dashboard.

- Adjust settings like brightness, temperature, or motion detection to confirm they're responding correctly.

With everything connected and functioning, you're ready to move on to automating your smart home!

Step 3: Setting Up Voice Assistants (Google Assistant & Alexa)

Adding a voice assistant to your smart home makes controlling devices even easier. With Google Assistant or Amazon Alexa, you can adjust lights, thermostats, and other smart gadgets using simple voice commands. Here's how to set them up with Home Assistant.

Setting Up Google Assistant

Google Assistant lets you control your smart home hands-free. Follow these steps to connect it to Home Assistant:

1. Add Google Assistant to Home Assistant

- Open Home Assistant on your computer or mobile device.
- Go to Settings > Integrations and search for Google Assistant.
- Select it and follow the on-screen instructions to complete the setup.
- You may need to enable specific APIs and services in the Google Cloud Console during the process.

2. Link Your Google Account

Sign in with your Google account when prompted.

Grant permission for Home Assistant to control your smart devices.

Once linked, Google Assistant can communicate with your devices.

3. Test Google Assistant

Try out a few voice commands to ensure everything is working properly:

- "Hey Google, turn on the living room lights."
- "Hey Google, set the thermostat to 72 degrees."
- "Hey Google, lock the front door."

If the setup was successful, Google Assistant will respond and carry out the command.

Setting Up Amazon Alexa

Alexa is another great option for hands-free smart home control. Here's how to connect it to Home Assistant:

1. Add Alexa to Home Assistant

- Open Home Assistant on your device.
- Go to Settings > Integrations and search for Amazon Alexa.
- Select it and follow the setup instructions.
- You may need to enable certain skills and cloud services in the Amazon Developer Console.

2. Link Your Amazon Account

Sign in with your Amazon account when prompted.

Approve the necessary permissions for Alexa to manage your smart devices.

Confirm which devices Alexa should be able to control, such as lights, locks, and thermostats.

3. Test Alexa

Once everything is set up, test Alexa with a few voice commands:

- "Alexa, turn off the bedroom lights."
- "Alexa, set the thermostat to 70 degrees."

- "Alexa, lock the front door."

By setting up Google Assistant or Alexa, you can manage your entire smart home with simple voice commands, making daily tasks even more convenient.

Step 4: Automating Your Smart Home with Custom Commands and Routines

Both Google Assistant and Amazon Alexa allow you to automate tasks by setting up custom voice commands and routines. This means you can create a single command to control multiple devices—like turning off all lights, adjusting the thermostat, and locking the doors before bedtime.

Creating Routines in Google Assistant

1. Open the Google Home app on your phone.

2. Access Routines by tapping your profile picture (top right) and selecting Assistant settings > Routines.

3. Create a New Routine by tapping Add a Routine.

4. Set a Trigger Phrase, such as "Goodnight" or "I'm home."

5. Choose Actions—for example, dimming the lights, setting the thermostat, and playing relaxing music.

6. Save the Routine. Now, whenever you say "Hey Google, goodnight," all the selected actions will happen automatically.

Creating Routines in Amazon Alexa

1. Open the Alexa app on your phone.

2. Go to Routines by tapping the menu (three lines in the top left) and selecting Routines.

3. Tap the + Button to start a new routine.

4. Choose a Trigger, such as a voice command ("Alexa, good morning") or a set time (e.g., 7:00 AM).

5. Add Actions—this could be turning on the lights, adjusting the thermostat, or playing a morning news briefing.

6. Save the Routine. Once set up, simply saying "Alexa, good morning" will activate all the linked actions.

Advanced Customization (Optional)

If you want even more control, both Google Assistant and Alexa offer additional customization options.

For Google Assistant:

- Use IFTTT (If This, Then That) – Set up complex automations that link multiple services and smart devices.
- Create Device Groups – Control multiple devices at once by grouping them (e.g., "Living Room Lights").

For Amazon Alexa:

Enable Alexa Skills – Access thousands of third-party skills to expand Alexa's capabilities.

Sync Music Across Rooms – Play the same music or podcast on multiple Alexa-enabled speakers throughout your home.

By setting up routines and custom commands, you can simplify daily tasks and make your smart home more convenient, letting your voice assistant handle multiple actions with a single command.

Step 5: Automating Your Smart Home for Effortless Control

Automation makes your smart home work for you by responding to specific events without requiring manual input.

Example: Hands-Free Lighting

1. Open Settings > Automations in Home Assistant and create a new automation.

2. Choose a Trigger, such as sunset, so your lights turn on automatically as it gets dark.

3. Set an Action to specify which lights should turn on and in which areas of your home.

Enhanced Security with Smart Alerts

- Use a motion sensor to detect movement when no one is home.
- Add a condition so alerts only activate when your home is set to Away Mode.

- Set an action to send a notification to your phone and turn on security cameras if motion is detected.

Smart Climate Control

Combine different factors, like temperature and humidity, to automatically adjust your HVAC system.

For example, if the room gets too hot and humid, your smart home can turn on the air conditioning or a fan to maintain comfort.

Step 6: Expanding Your Smart Home with Sensors and Relays

Adding sensors and relays helps your home respond more intelligently to changes in the environment.

Temperature and Humidity Control

Install a DHT22 sensor to monitor room conditions.

Set up automations that turn on a fan or humidifier if the temperature or humidity reaches a certain level.

Door and Window Alerts

Place door and window sensors to receive instant alerts if they are opened unexpectedly.

Use them to adjust heating and cooling—for example, turning off the heater when a window is left open.

Smartening Up Regular Appliances

Connect everyday appliances like fans or coffee makers to smart relays.

This lets you control them remotely through Home Assistant, just like any other smart device.

By automating tasks and adding smart sensors, your home can adapt to your lifestyle, making it more efficient, secure, and convenient.

Step 7: Controlling Your Smart Home from Anywhere

Being able to access your smart home remotely gives you both convenience and peace of mind. Here's how you can set it up:

Easy Remote Access with Home Assistant Cloud

Home Assistant offers a cloud service that simplifies remote access for a small monthly fee.

To activate it, go to Settings > Home Assistant Cloud and sign up.

Free Option: Port Forwarding

If you prefer a no-cost alternative, you can use port forwarding on your router.

This method allows you to connect to Home Assistant when you're away from home.

Security Tip: Since port forwarding can be risky, use strong passwords or consider a VPN for added security.

Smartphone Control on the Go

Install the Home Assistant mobile app to manage your devices, receive notifications, and control automations from anywhere.

This ensures you're always connected to your smart home, no matter where you are.

Step 8: Simplifying Smart Home Management with a Custom Dashboard

A well-organized dashboard makes it easy to control and monitor your home at a glance.

Customize Your Layout

Head to Settings > Dashboards and arrange your devices, sensors, and automations using the drag-and-drop feature.

Organize by Room

Create separate views for different areas of your home so you can quickly access only the devices that matter in each space.

Quick Access Buttons

Add widgets and shortcuts for frequently used actions, such as a "Turn Off All Lights" button for bedtime.

Stay Informed with Notifications

Set up alerts for important events, like open doors or unusual temperature changes, so you're always aware of what's happening in your home.

Creating a Smarter, More Connected Home

With Raspberry Pi 5 and Home Assistant, you can build a fully customizable smart home system tailored to your needs. From automating routines to integrating voice assistants, this guide covers the basics to get you started.

For more detailed instructions, Google's official documentation provides step-by-step guidance on connecting Google Assistant, setting up custom actions, and optimizing your smart home experience.

AUTOMATING TASKS WITH PYTHON

AI and Machine Learning are no longer just for high-end computers. With the Raspberry Pi 5, you can dive into AI projects from the comfort of your home—whether you're a hobbyist, student, or developer looking for an affordable way to experiment.

Why Use Raspberry Pi 5 for AI and ML?

The Raspberry Pi 5 comes with major improvements over previous versions, making it more capable of handling AI tasks:

✔️ **Faster Performance** – A quad-core Cortex-A76 processor (2.4GHz) boosts speed and efficiency.

✔️ **More Memory** – Available in 4GB and 8GB versions for smoother model execution.

✔️ **PCIe Support** – Enables faster storage and the use of AI accelerators for better performance.

✔️ **Enhanced Graphics –** The VideoCore VII GPU improves image processing and lightweight ML workloads.

✔️ **Budget-Friendly –** A fraction of the cost of traditional AI hardware, making it a great option for learning and prototyping.

Although it's not meant to replace powerful AI workstations, the Raspberry Pi 5 is an excellent low-cost platform for small-scale AI applications and experimentation.

What You Need to Get Started

Before setting up your Raspberry Pi 5 for AI projects, make sure you have:

✔️ Raspberry Pi 5 (4GB or 8GB RAM recommended)

✔️ Power Adapter (USB-C, 5V, 5A)

✔️ MicroSD Card (At least 32GB for the OS and AI models)

✔️ External SSD (Optional – For faster data processing)

✔️ Camera Module (Optional – Useful for image recognition projects)

✔️ USB AI Accelerator (Optional – Google Coral TPU or Intel Movidius can enhance AI performance)

✔️ Internet Connection (Required for software installation and downloading AI models)

Step 1: Setting Up Your Raspberry Pi 5 for AI and ML

1. Install Raspberry Pi OS (64-bit)

To get the best performance, use the 64-bit version of Raspberry Pi OS.

Download the 64-bit Raspberry Pi OS from the official website.

Use Raspberry Pi Imager to write it to your microSD card.

Insert the microSD card into your Raspberry Pi, power it on, and update the system:

```bash
sudo apt update && sudo apt upgrade -y
```

2. Install Python and AI/ML Libraries

Since Python is the go-to language for AI and ML, install the necessary tools:

```bash
sudo apt update && sudo apt upgrade -y
sudo apt install python3-pip -y
pip3 install numpy pandas matplotlib opencv-python tflite-runtime
```

✔ NumPy & Pandas – Helps with handling and processing data efficiently.

✔ Matplotlib – Useful for creating charts and visualizing data.

✔ TensorFlow Lite – A lightweight AI framework designed to run ML models on Raspberry Pi.

✔ OpenCV – Essential for image processing and computer vision tasks.

These libraries are the building blocks of AI projects on Raspberry Pi 5, helping you work with data, images, and machine learning models.

With Raspberry Pi 5, you can start exploring AI and ML right away—whether you want to build image recognition systems, analyze data, or automate tasks. As you grow, you can add AI accelerators and fine-tune your setup for even better performance.

Step 2: Running AI and Machine Learning Models on Raspberry Pi 5

Now that your Raspberry Pi 5 is set up, let's explore how to run AI and machine learning models. We'll start with image classification using TensorFlow Lite and then move on to real-time face detection with OpenCV.

1. Running a Pre-Trained AI Model with TensorFlow Lite

You can test your Raspberry Pi 5's AI capabilities by running a pre-trained image recognition model with TensorFlow Lite.

Step 1: Download a Sample AI Model

First, download a pre-trained image classification model by running:

```bash
wget https://your-model-url.com/model.tflite
```

Step 2: Run the Model Using Python

Next, use the following Python script to load the model, process an image, and make a prediction:

```python
import tensorflow.lite as tflite
import numpy as np
from PIL import Image
# Load the TensorFlow Lite model
model_path = "mobilenet_v2_1.0_224_inat_bird_quant.tflite"
interpreter = tflite.Interpreter(model_path=model_path)
interpreter.allocate_tensors()
# Prepare the input image
input_details = interpreter.get_input_details()
output_details = interpreter.get_output_details()
image = Image.open("test_image.jpg").resize((224, 224))
input_data = np.expand_dims(np.array(image, dtype=np.float32) / 255.0, axis=0)
# Run the model
interpreter.set_tensor(input_details[0]['index'], input_data)
interpreter.invoke()
output_data = interpreter.get_tensor(output_details[0]['index'])
print("Prediction:", output_data)
```

- ◆ What This Does:
  - Loads a pre-trained AI model for image classification.
  - Processes an image and converts it into a format the model can understand.
  - Runs the model and prints a prediction based on the image.

This is a great way to experiment with AI on Raspberry Pi 5, especially if you're interested in image recognition or smart applications.

2. Real-Time Face Detection with OpenCV and a Camera

If you have a camera module, you can use OpenCV to detect faces in real time.

Step 1: Install OpenCV

First, install OpenCV by running:

```bash
pip install opencv-python
```

Step 2: Run a Face Detection Script

Now, use this Python script to detect faces using your Pi camera:

```python
import cv2
# Load OpenCV's built-in face detection model
face_cascade = cv2.CascadeClassifier(cv2.data.haarcascades +
"haarcascade_frontalface_default.xml")


# Access the camera
cap = cv2.VideoCapture(0, cv2.CAP_V4L2)
while True:
  ret, frame = cap.read()
  gray = cv2.cvtColor(frame, cv2.COLOR_BGR2GRAY)
```

```
    faces = face_cascade.detectMultiScale(gray, 1.1, 4)

    for (x, y, w, h) in faces:

        cv2.rectangle(frame, (x, y), (x+w, y+h), (255, 0, 0), 2)

    cv2.imshow("Face Detection", frame)

    if cv2.waitKey(1) & 0xFF == ord("q"):

        break

cap.release()

cv2.destroyAllWindows()
```
```

- **How It Works:**

  - Uses OpenCV's built-in face detection model.

  - Captures video from the Pi Camera.

  - Detects faces in real time and highlights them with a bounding box.

This is a fun and practical project that can be used for security systems, smart mirrors, or AI-powered applications.

By running these AI projects, you can start exploring artificial intelligence on Raspberry Pi 5 and build exciting applications like object recognition, smart surveillance, or AI-powered assistants!

## Step 3: Running AI and Machine Learning on Raspberry Pi 5

Now that your Raspberry Pi 5 is set up, let's put it to use by running AI and machine learning models. We'll start by using a pre-trained model to classify images and then move on to real-time face detection using OpenCV and a camera module.

### 1. Running a Pre-Trained AI Model with TensorFlow Lite

One of the easiest ways to experiment with AI on your Raspberry Pi 5 is by using a pre-trained image classification model. This allows your device to recognize and categorize objects in pictures.
```

Step 1: Download a Sample Model

First, download a sample AI model by running the following command in your terminal:

```bash
wget https://your-model-url.com/model.tflite
```

Step 2: Process an Image and Get a Prediction

Next, use this Python script to load the model, process an image, and make a prediction:

```python
import tensorflow.lite as tflite
import numpy as np
from PIL import Image
# Load the AI model
model_path = "mobilenet_v2_1.0_224_inat_bird_quant.tflite"
interpreter = tflite.Interpreter(model_path=model_path)
interpreter.allocate_tensors()
# Prepare the input image
input_details = interpreter.get_input_details()
output_details = interpreter.get_output_details()
image = Image.open("test_image.jpg").resize((224, 224))
input_data = np.expand_dims(np.array(image, dtype=np.float32) / 255.0, axis=0)
# Run the model and get a prediction
interpreter.set_tensor(input_details[0]['index'], input_data)
interpreter.invoke()
output_data = interpreter.get_tensor(output_details[0]['index'])
print("Prediction:", output_data)
```

What This Does:

- Loads a pre-trained AI model onto your Raspberry Pi.
- Processes an image to match the model's input requirements.
- Runs the AI model and prints a prediction about what the image contains.

This is a great way to explore AI on Raspberry Pi 5, whether you're working on image recognition, smart applications, or automation projects.

2. Detecting Faces in Real-Time with OpenCV and a Camera

If you have a camera module, you can use OpenCV to detect faces in real time. This is perfect for projects like security cameras, smart assistants, or interactive AI systems.

Step 1: Install OpenCV

Before running the script, install OpenCV by typing this in your terminal:

```bash
pip install opencv-python
```

Step 2: Run the Face Detection Script

Now, use this Python script to capture video and detect faces:

```python
import cv2
# Load OpenCV's face detection model
face_cascade = cv2.CascadeClassifier(cv2.data.haarcascades + "haarcascade_frontalface_default.xml")
# Open the camera
cap = cv2.VideoCapture(0, cv2.CAP_V4L2)
while True:
    ret, frame = cap.read()
    gray = cv2.cvtColor(frame, cv2.COLOR_BGR2GRAY)
```

```
    faces = face_cascade.detectMultiScale(gray, 1.1, 4)

    for (x, y, w, h) in faces:

        cv2.rectangle(frame, (x, y), (x+w, y+h), (255, 0, 0), 2)

    cv2.imshow("Face Detection", frame)

    if cv2.waitKey(1) & 0xFF == ord("q"):

        break

cap.release()

cv2.destroyAllWindows()
```
```

**How This Works:**

- Uses OpenCV's pre-trained face detection model.

- Captures live video from the Pi Camera.

- Detects faces and highlights them with a blue rectangle.

This project is a great introduction to computer vision and can be adapted for various AI-powered applications.

With these projects, you're getting hands-on experience with machine learning on Raspberry Pi 5. Whether you're interested in image recognition, smart security, or automation, this setup is a solid foundation for your AI journey!

# CHAPTER 6

# MEDIA AND ENTERTAINMENT PROJECTS

Turn Your Raspberry Pi 5 into a Media Player – Featured in MagPi Issue 142

Looking for an affordable way to organize and enjoy your movie collection? The latest MagPi Magazine (Issue 142) has a guide on how to build your own Raspberry Pi 5 media
```

player. With powerful hardware and flexible storage options, the Raspberry Pi 5 is a great choice for creating a custom home entertainment system.

Why Choose the Raspberry Pi 5 for a Media Player?

The Raspberry Pi 5 is packed with features that make it perfect for handling media files. It supports PCI-express storage, meaning you can connect an M.2 SSD drive for faster speeds and more storage. This means smoother playback and better performance, even with high-resolution videos.

What You Can Do with Your Raspberry Pi 5 Media Player

By setting up a Raspberry Pi 5 media player, you can:

- Manage and play your movie collection with ease.
- Enjoy smooth video playback thanks to the fast processor and SSD storage.
- Stream movies and shows from services like Netflix, Hulu, and Amazon Prime Video.
- Discover public domain films and classic movies you won't find on mainstream platforms.
- Explore homebrew games, opening up a world of unique indie titles.

What You'll Need to Get Started

To build your media player, you'll need:

- A Raspberry Pi 5
- An M.2 SSD drive (for storage)
- A power adapter
- An HDMI cable (to connect to a TV)
- A case and cooling system (optional, but recommended)

Prices for the Raspberry Pi 5 and accessories vary, so it's worth checking different retailers for deals. Some stores sell bundles with everything you need, including power adapters, remote controls, and cables, which can help you save money.

Other Cool Raspberry Pi 5 Projects in MagPi 142

Besides building a media player, MagPi 142 also showcases other fun and creative Raspberry Pi projects:

- **DIY Synthesizer** – Recreate the iconic Yamaha DX7 sound using the Mini Dexed software.

- **Cat TV** – Set up a mini television for your cat with videos of birds and fish.

- **Robot Arm Control** – Use a Wii remote to control a robotic arm with motion gestures.

- **Data Recovery Tool** – Retrieve old files from floppy disks and CDs to preserve important data.

ADDING STREAMING SERVICES AND LOCAL MEDIA

Once Kodi is installed, you can start adding your favorite content. If you have movies or TV shows saved on an external drive, just plug it in, and Kodi will automatically organize everything for you.

If you prefer streaming, Kodi has official add-ons for platforms like YouTube and Netflix. Some services may require extra setup, but once configured, you'll have access to a wide range of content.

For those with a home server or NAS (Network-Attached Storage), Kodi can connect directly to your media library, letting you stream content without needing to transfer files manually. If you're looking for a more refined way to manage your collection, Plex is another great option.

Making Navigation Easier

While a keyboard and mouse are useful during setup, a remote makes everyday navigation much easier. If your TV supports HDMI-CEC, you can use your regular TV remote to control Kodi—no extra hardware required. You can also turn your smartphone into a Kodi remote by installing the Kore app.

For those who prefer a more tactile experience, a compact wireless keyboard with a built-in touchpad is a great choice. It's easy to use and makes searching for content much faster than using an on-screen keyboard.

Troubleshooting Common Issues

Even with a smooth setup, small issues can sometimes arise:

Videos keep buffering or stuttering? Check your internet connection and ensure hardware acceleration is enabled in the settings.

Device overheating? Using a cooling fan can help keep the temperature down.

System feeling slow? A fresh install or lowering the resolution to 1080p instead of 4K can improve performance.

Setting up a media center with a Raspberry Pi 5 is simpler than you might expect. It's a cost-effective way to create a powerful, customizable streaming system that can even handle light gaming. Plus, it's easy to upgrade or modify whenever needed.

BUILDING A MEDIA CENTER WITH KODI

Turning a Raspberry Pi into a media center with Kodi is a simple, affordable, and highly functional project. With Kodi, you can stream content from various services or play your personal collection of movies, TV shows, music, and photos. This guide will walk you through everything you need to know—from choosing the right Kodi operating system to adding streaming services, importing local files, and setting up network access.

WHAT IS KODI AND WHY USE IT?

Kodi is a free, open-source media player that was originally developed as Xbox Media Center (XBMC) for the first-generation Xbox. Over time, it evolved into a widely used app that runs on Linux, Windows, macOS, Android, and even smart TVs.

Since Kodi is open-source, developers have created lightweight, specialized operating systems like LibreELEC, OpenELEC, and Xbian. These versions are optimized for media playback and boot directly into Kodi for a seamless home theater experience.

Kodi offers two main features:

1. Playing local files – You can watch movies, TV shows, and listen to music stored on a USB drive or network server.

2. Streaming through add-ons – Kodi supports add-ons for services like Netflix, YouTube, Plex, Funimation, and Spotify, giving you access to a wide range of content.

Additionally, Kodi can even be used for retro gaming, allowing you to play classic games using emulators.

Why Use a Raspberry Pi for Kodi?

The Raspberry Pi is an excellent choice for a media center because it's small, energy-efficient, and powerful enough to run Kodi smoothly. You can use it to play files directly from a USB drive or stream content from a network storage device. Plus, with Kodi's extensive add-on library, you can access tons of entertainment without needing expensive hardware.

Which Raspberry Pi Model Should You Use for Kodi?

Kodi works well on almost any Raspberry Pi, even the budget-friendly Pi Zero. However, the best choice depends on your needs:

- Raspberry Pi 4,pi 5 – The best overall option, capable of playing 4K video at 60 FPS.

- Raspberry Pi 3 B+ – A solid choice for 1080p playback and general streaming.

- Raspberry Pi Zero / Zero W – A budget-friendly option for creating a compact streaming device.

For most people, the Raspberry Pi 4 is the best choice, especially if you want to stream in 4K. If you're fine with 1080p, the Pi 3 B+ is a great alternative. And if you're looking for the cheapest solution, the Pi Zero is a good way to build a portable, USB-powered streaming stick.

With Kodi on a Raspberry Pi, you get a flexible and powerful media center without the high cost of commercial streaming devices. It's easy to set up, upgrade, and customize, making it a great project for any entertainment enthusiast.

Choosing the Right Operating System for Your Kodi Media Center

Setting up a Kodi media center on a Raspberry Pi starts with selecting the right operating system (OS). You have two main options:

1. Kodi as an App – You can install Kodi on a general-purpose OS like Linux or Android. This allows you to use your Raspberry Pi for more than just media playback, such as web browsing and productivity tasks.

2. Dedicated Kodi OS – If you want a device that functions purely as a media center, a standalone Kodi OS is the best choice.

For those interested in retro gaming, some gaming OS options like RetroPie, Recalbox, and Batocera also come with Kodi built-in.

Best Standalone Kodi Operating Systems

If you want a dedicated media center, these are the top choices:

LibreELEC – The best option overall, supporting 4K playback at 60 FPS and compatible with the Raspberry Pi 4.

OSMC – A user-friendly choice with strong community support. OSMC even offers its own pre-configured Kodi device, the Vero 4K. However, it does not yet support the Raspberry Pi 4.

XBian – Ideal for users who want the latest updates and features, as it offers frequent software updates and useful pre-installed tools like VNC and Samba.

Using a Retro Gaming OS with Kodi

If you're into gaming, you can install Kodi within a retro gaming OS so you can enjoy both media playback and gaming on the same device. Here are the best options:

RetroPie – The most customizable option, perfect for experienced users who want to tweak settings and add extra features.

Recalbox – A beginner-friendly option that includes gamepad support right out of the box, making setup easier.

Batocera – Similar to Recalbox, offering a simple and easy-to-use interface for those new to gaming and media centers.

Running Kodi as an App

For a more flexible setup, you can install Kodi as an app on a full-featured operating system like Debian, Ubuntu, Raspbian, or Android. This way, your Raspberry Pi can function as both a regular computer and a media center.

A great choice for this approach is RaspEX, a Debian-based OS that comes with Kodi pre-installed, along with legal streaming add-ons like Netflix and Plex.

Note; For a dedicated media center: LibreELEC is the best overall choice.

For a mix of gaming and media streaming: RetroPie is best for advanced users, while Recalbox and Batocera are great for beginners.

For a multi-purpose device: Install Kodi as an app on Linux or Android.

Choosing the right OS will help you create the perfect Kodi setup for your needs!

INSTALLING KODI ON A RASPBERRY PI 5

When the Raspberry Pi 5 came out, I thought it was a perfect chance to upgrade my old quad-core Intel Celeron media machine. The specs appeared perfect for a home theater system, and I had already splurged on a Nvidia quad HDMI PCIe 1x card for my current setup. But having had problems with drivers on Ubuntu, my setup failed totally. Despite replacing the power supply, I couldn't get it working.

Instead of continuing to troubleshoot, I decided to proceed with a fresh approach. I purchased an 8GB Raspberry Pi 5 from Cool Components and set it up within a few hours using LibreELEC.

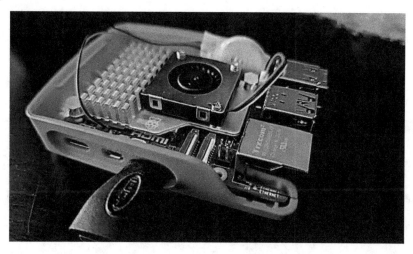

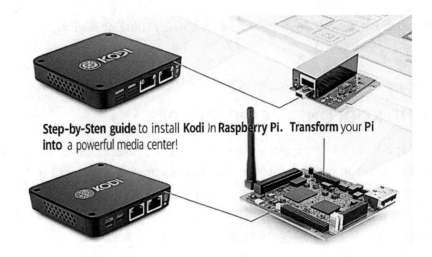

Step-by-Sten guide to install **Kodi**)n **Raspberry Pi. Transform** your **Pi into** a powerful media center!

Upgrading the Setup

Although the vanilla case works, it is not appropriate for my installation—it looks too small for the space behind my TV. I plan on modifying the case so that it can be more useful to my needs. I would like to get 4K H.265 HEVC playback onto my TV and projector. I will need to replace my first-generation smart TV, however, before I can fully utilize this.

My Kodi Setup Journey

Installing Kodi on the Raspberry Pi 5 has been a task. I started off with the stable 32-bit LibreELEC build, which was fine initially. I subsequently, though, switched to the 64-bit nightly edition for better performance. I had a go at OSMC as well, but due to its lack of updates and Raspberry Pi 5 support, it was not an option for me. Finally, I installed the official Raspberry Pi OS (Raspbian) and installed Kodi manually.

Kodi on TV and Projector

I initially believed that I would be able to mirror Kodi on both my TV and projector since many users possess dual 4K screens with high refresh rates. However, LibreELEC does not support it at all. I was able to get dual display output to function in Raspbian, but Kodi would not mirror correctly. I searched around for some solutions, and I soon learned that the most straightforward way to solve it was to use an HDMI splitter. I acquired a powered one which suited my needs, albeit that it required a USB port for power.

Audio Challenges: AC3, DTS, and Surround Sound

Having multichannel audio capabilities was likely the most infuriating part of the installation. I had been hoping to finally experience DTS, AAC, and DTS Master Audio on my Onkyo 7.1 surround sound receiver through HDMI. While Dolby Digital/AC3 was fine, connecting the Pi directly to my receiver would sometimes result in my TV shutting off randomly due to an issue with remote input signals not being properly passed.

To circumvent this, I also considered disabling standby modes, but the bigger problem was lack of DTS and other high-quality sound support. To bypass it, I acquired an USB sound card connected to the system with optical out and 8-channel analog out, which allows future-proofing for potential 7.1 audio expansion. Once I configured things through Kodi settings, it worked as intended at last.

One of the best features of this setup is how easy it is to create and transition among multiple SD card versions. Whenever a new version comes out, I can simply create a new SD card and transfer my files into the home directory. In fact, just two days ago, a promising new version came out, and I will most likely try it out soon by installing another SD card.

Overall, things are fine with my setup, and things will improve with Raspberry Pi 5 development continuing.

Fixing the TV Standby Problem

I discovered that the TV standby problem was caused by the CEC adapter, which is enabled by default in the Raspberry Pi but was not present on my old Kodi box. Thankfully, I was able to turn it off by navigating to:

Settings > System > Input > Peripherals > Additional Devices > CEC Adapter

Having this issue resolved, I now have my Raspberry Pi 5 plugged directly into my Onkyo receiver, as well as my Chromecast.

Next Steps for Audio and HDMI Setup

Once I have HDMI audio correctly configured, I can now remove the external sound card. I'm also curious about moving the HDMI splitter to the receiver output, but I should research what that would do to the Freeview HD signal via the TV's ARC (Audio Return Channel).

In all honesty, my antenna hasn't worked for months—most likely even a whole year—so it may not be a factor anyway.

Conclusion

It has been a frustrating but rewarding experience to install Kodi on a Raspberry Pi 5. While video playback is excellent, dual display support was an issue, and audio output required special hardware. But with some additions—like a sturdier case, an HDMI splitter, and an external sound card—the installation is now a good home media system.

STREAMING GAMES AND EMULATION

The Raspberry Pi 5 has arrived, and it's making waves in the retro gaming community. This latest version of the popular mini-computer comes packed with powerful upgrades, making it an excellent choice for those who love classic games. Despite its small size, it delivers impressive performance improvements that enhance the gaming experience.

A Powerful Upgrade

At its core, the Raspberry Pi 5 is powered by a quad-core Broadcom ARM v8 Cortex-A76 processor running at 2.4 GHz. If you need more speed, you can overclock it up to 3.1 GHz. It also features a Broadcom VideoCore 7 GPU that supports 4K video at 60 frames per second, making it great for both gaming and media streaming.

Since overclocking pushes the hardware harder, using an active cooling system is a smart choice to keep temperatures in check. The Raspberry Pi 5 comes in two versions: a 4 GB RAM model for $59.99 and an 8 GB RAM model for $79.99, so you can pick the one that best suits your needs and budget.

Turning the Raspberry Pi 5 Into a Retro Gaming Console

One of the most exciting uses for the Raspberry Pi 5 is running classic games through emulation. Thanks to its upgraded hardware, it can now handle more demanding systems that older models struggled with, like the GameCube, Nintendo Wii, Nintendo Switch, and PlayStation 2.

For example, Sega Saturn games now run at a smooth 60 frames per second with no tweaks needed, showing just how much performance has improved.

Emulation Performance

When using the Dolphin emulator to play GameCube games, performance varies—some games run great, while others may experience slowdowns. The same goes for PlayStation 2 emulation, where results depend on the game and settings. However, Dreamcast and PSP games generally run well, though the most demanding titles can push the hardware to its limits.

Arcade emulation is another strong area for the Raspberry Pi 5. Games like Killer Instinct and the Cave CV1000 series of bullet hell shooters run smoothly, with only minor hiccups here and there. Given its affordability, this little device delivers an impressive balance of power and cost for retro gaming fans.

More Than Just Gaming

The Raspberry Pi 5 isn't just for gaming—it's a versatile tool for all kinds of projects. Whether you're building a desktop PC, a tablet, or a dedicated gaming console, it serves as a solid foundation. With add-ons like SSD storage and custom cases, you can tailor it to fit your needs.

For those looking to explore game emulation, the Raspberry Pi 5 offers an incredible combination of nostalgia and modern performance. It's an affordable, compact, and capable option for both long-time gamers and newcomers alike.

Here is a paraphrased and rewritten version of the content, reorganized in order from 1 to 5 for easier reading and understanding:

RANKING THE TOP EMULATION PLATFORMS FOR THE RASPBERRY PI 5

Classic game emulation is among the most universal uses of the Raspberry Pi. There are plenty of emulators available, with users able to play old classics from throughout many generations of console. The Raspberry Pi 5 takes this to the next level, with the ability to have five dedicated emulation platforms supported—not having to install different programs for each console anymore.

However, each platform comes with its own strengths and weaknesses, making it difficult to choose the best one. To help, I've ranked the five major emulation platforms based on their user interface, ease of setup, compatible consoles, performance, controller support, and additional features.

It's important to note that while the Raspberry Pi 5 has been available for almost a year, software support remains inconsistent. Some emulators are still experiencing an issue with the Bookworm version of Raspberry Pi OS. A platform that is ranked lower on this list due to some compatibility issues with the Raspberry Pi 5 might run extremely well on older versions. All tests were conducted using the latest stable releases of each emulator, so beta functionality is not included.

1. Batocera – The Most Feature-Rich Emulation Platform

Why It's Best: Batocera is the best because it is highly featured with a wide range of compatibility with consoles.

While its user interface might be termed flashy when compared to the rest, Batocera delivers where it matters. It comes with top-shelf features such as multiple controllers (8-player) support and built-in Kodi for playback, in addition to Moonlight streaming for gaming over the internet. You can even stream games to Batocera directly with a Sunshine host running on your network.

Similar to Recalbox and Lakka, Batocera has LAN file transferring support, although games need to be stored in their respective console directories in order to show up in the system. In performance, it plays PSP, GameCube, Nintendo DS, and PlayStation 1 games effortlessly.

But a couple of cores have some minor issues. The Wii emulator (Dolphin) fails to recognize certain controllers in wired mode and wireless mode, but one may assist it with manual configuration file adjustments. While Batocera previously supported a PlayStation 2 core, the latter is no longer supported in the latest version.

Despite these minor glitches, Batocera remains the overall best emulation platform for the Raspberry Pi 5 due to its feature set and wide compatibility.

2. Lakka – Best for Newbies

Why It's Second: Lakka has a simple, PlayStation-like interface that new users can easily understand.

Lakka was not for me originally, perhaps because it lacks a web UI or Kodi support. However, having used it for a while, I realize that it offers the best interface for new users. Menus are nicely organized, and one plus over all other platforms, it does not require you to manually sort ROMs by putting them in individual folders, but rather put them straight inside the ROMs folder via File Explorer.

Its only small drawback is its native Japanese controller mapping, which reverses B/O and A/X buttons. Luckily, this can be remapped in settings.

Lakka provides great performance for more demanding systems such as PlayStation 1, PSP, GameCube, DS, and Wii. It even has a PlayStation 2 core (Play!), although in my testing it was not usable.

If you're looking for an easy-to-use platform with solid compatibility, Lakka is a fantastic choice—though it lacks the extra features found in Batocera.

3. RECALBOX – THE BEST USER INTERFACE

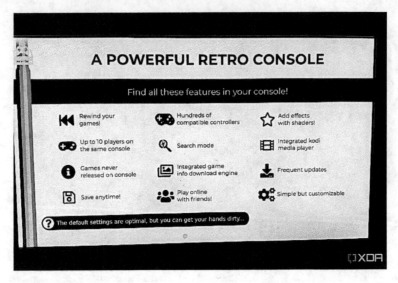

Why It's Ranked Third: Recalbox offers an intuitive, well-designed UI and comes preloaded with games, but lacks Wii, GameCube, and DS support.

Although ranked third, Recalbox is still a solid choice for retro gamers. The initial booting process is a bit longer than that of some of the other platforms, but once it's done with that, you're greeted with what I think is the most visually appealing UI of any Raspberry Pi emulator. It strikes a perfect balance between RetroPie's retro aesthetic and Batocera's flashy looks, being soft on the eyes while still easy to navigate.

Recalbox has web UI access, which means users can transfer games over a local network. It also includes Kodi, so you can use your Raspberry Pi as a media center as well as an emulation monster. The platform supports Nintendo 64, PlayStation 1, and PSP games nicely and supports up to 10 controllers (with extra USB hubs).

But its lack of including the right cores for Wii, GameCube, and Nintendo DS prevents it from being further up. Included in future releases, Recalbox would already be on the top two.

4. RetroPie – Best for Older Raspberry Pi Models

Why It's Ranked Fourth: RetroPie is an excellent emulator—except for the Raspberry Pi 5.

My go-to emulator previously was RetroPie when I was working with a Raspberry Pi Zero. Given the power of the Raspberry Pi 5, my expectations were high, but unfortunately, RetroPie is lacking with this new hardware.

The biggest issue is the lack of a proper Raspberry Pi 5 image. The users are forced to compile RetroPie manually through a set of rather complex terminal commands, and this takes hours even on the 8GB model. The latest version of RetroPie also only supports a limited number of cores.

On the up side, it's possible for users to dual-boot RetroPie with Raspberry Pi OS, and the UI is prettier than RetroArch. While my own attempts at sideloading a PSP core did not work out, others claim to have succeeded in playing Wii games. GBA, SNES, and early Atari work wonderfully, and user scripts provide a way of adding more emulators.

If the ranking was among x86-based SBCs or mini-PCs, RetroPie would have come so much higher. But on the Raspberry Pi 5, it's trailing behind the pack.

5. RetroArch – The Hardest to Configure

Why It's Last: A few cores and a brutal setup process render RetroArch the weakest in the lineup.

Despite being one of the most popular emulation platforms, RetroArch's implementation on the Raspberry Pi 5 is disappointing. One of its strongest points is that it may be installed on top of a current OS, rather than having to flash an image onto a microSD card.

But this advantage is marred by a convoluted installation process. Even when successfully installed, RetroArch is hampered by the absence of ARM64 cores. A lot of old consoles are not supported, and some cores, such as the PSX emulator, do not even load any games.

While RetroArch allows retro gaming without ever having to change microSD cards, it not being able to emulate Wii, PSX, or PSP games makes it a lesser choice for most users.

PlayStation 2 Emulation?

If the user wants to play PlayStation 2 games on the Raspberry Pi 5, options are scarce. None of the popular emulators support playing PS2 games, but there is a hack-around.

The late AetherSX2, an Android emulator for the PS2, can indeed be used on the Raspberry Pi 5 with LineageOS. It can be installed by downloading older AetherSX2 versions from the Internet Archive and installing it after flashing LineageOS on your device. Performance is spotty, however, and only a handful of games will work properly—especially on the 8GB model.

If you're determined to play PS2 games, you'll need to manage your expectations.

Final Thoughts

For the best all-around emulation experience on the Raspberry Pi 5, Batocera takes the win due to its rich feature set and wide compatibility. Lakka is easiest to use for beginners, while Recalbox offers the most polished UI. RetroPie is still a decent option for legacy Raspberry Pi hardware but has problems with the Raspberry Pi 5. RetroArch, although popular, is last due to its complex setup and limited game library.

CREATING A HOME AUDIO SYSTEM

Creating a Small Multi-Channel Digital Audio Workstation (DAW) using Raspberry Pi

When you hear the words digital audio workstation (DAW), you might imagine a powerful computer with a large mixing board hooked up to it or an external sound card. But do you need to spend all that cash on all that gear? What if you could create a seriously powerful, multi-channel recording and editing station out of a Raspberry Pi—at a fraction of the cost?

While the Raspberry Pi 5 isn't as powerful as a desktop machine or a high-end MacBook, this level of processing power isn't always necessary. For most audio projects, open-source tools in the form of Audacity on a Pi 5 will suffice. Through this tutorial, we will be guiding you through how to set up a tiny multi-channel DAW using the Raspberry Pi.

Important Notes

This handbook is provided in an informal nature, and we cannot guarantee support with future versions of Raspberry Pi OS or Audacity. You may have to adapt based on software updates. We do not offer individual assistance with this configuration, though you may post queries within our forums.

What You'll Need: Hardware Requirements

To work with multiple audio channels, you'll need the following components:

Raspberry Pi 5 – The 4GB model is fine for most setups, but if you're working on more complex projects, the 8GB or 16GB version is a better choice.

HiFiBerry DAC8x – A high-quality digital-to-analog converter for playback.

HiFiBerry ADC8x – An analog-to-digital converter for recording.

If you do not need multi-channel support, some of the other HiFiBerry sound cards such as the DAC2 ADC Pro or the Studio DAC/ADC will do just as well for your needs.

Getting Your Raspberry Pi Set Up

To get started, install the full version of Raspberry Pi OS, which includes a graphical user interface (GUI) required for running audio software. You'll also need to configure the sound interface properly—check the official HiFiBerry documentation for detailed setup instructions.

Once your Raspberry Pi is up and running, confirm that it recognizes your sound card by running these commands in the terminal:

```sh
aplay -l
arecord -l
```

If everything is set up correctly, you should see your HiFiBerry sound card listed for both playback and recording.

Installing and Configuring Audacity

To install Audacity on your Raspberry Pi:

1. Click the menu button in the top-left corner.

2. Open the Add/Remove Software tool.

3. Search for Audacity and install it.

After installation, you'll have a lightweight, multi-channel DAW in your hands!

From there, you can start experimenting with multi-track recording, editing, and mixing—all on a compact, affordable setup powered by the Raspberry Pi 5.

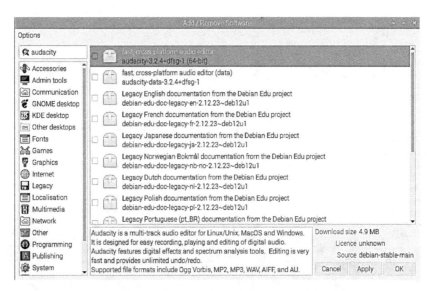

After installing Audacity, you'll need to configure it to work with your HiFiBerry sound card. Open Audio Setup and select hw:0,0 (or another ID if you haven't disabled the built-in sound). This ensures Audacity communicates directly with your sound card, avoiding unnecessary processing.

To prevent issues, it's a good idea to disable audio middleware like PipeWire or PulseAudio, as they can interfere with Audacity's performance.

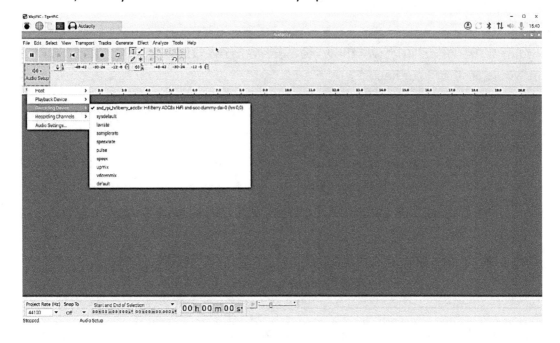

Testing Audacity

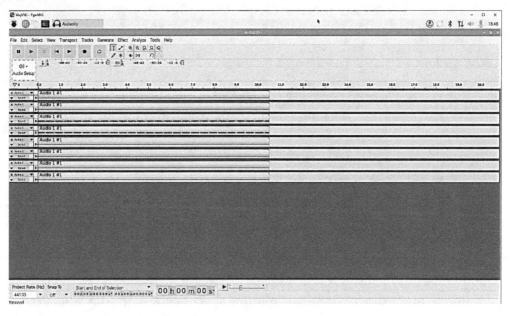

To check if everything is working, simply press the record button in Audacity.

If set up correctly, Audacity should start recording on all 8 channels.

Once recorded, press stop, rewind to the beginning, and hit play to listen back.

From here, you can explore Audacity's tools, effects, and filters to fine-tune your recordings. There's no strict workflow—experiment, read the documentation, and find what works best for your needs.

Things to Keep in Mind

While this setup is affordable and compact, it does come with some trade-offs:

- Limited Processing Power – Audacity and Raspberry Pi may not be suited for very complex projects.

- Small Audio Jacks – The 3.5mm ports may require adapter cables for some setups.

- Microphone Compatibility – The ADC8x isn't designed for direct microphone input, so you'll need an external preamp if you're using a mic.

Despite these limitations, this setup is a great way to build a budget-friendly, multi-channel recording system. Now, it's time to start creating!

CHAPTER 7

TROUBLESHOOTING AND ADVANCED TIPS

Troubleshooting Raspberry Pi 5 Boot Issues

Problem Description

A user tried accidentally to boot their new Raspberry Pi 5 with an SD card that was running DietPi for the Raspberry Pi 4. Not surprisingly, it wouldn't boot. However, after this attempt, the Pi wouldn't boot at all and displayed a blinking LED pattern of four long blinks and five short blinks—an error code for a bootloader issue.

After having successfully flashed the bootloader to an SD card and obtained a green screen, the user found that the Pi still would not boot from USB or SD and returned to the same flashing error pattern.

Community Suggestions & Troubleshooting Steps

1. Check for Corrupted Boot Media

   Booting with the wrong OS may have corrupted the SD card.

2. Follow Official Bootloader Recovery Guide

   A guide to debugging Raspberry Pi boot issues was suggested by one of the forum members.

3. Use New SD Card with Raspberry Pi OS

   The majority of boot problems are resolved by putting in a new, known-good SD card with Raspberry Pi OS and an official power supply.

Troubleshooting Attempts by User

Power Supply: Was using a 27W adapter bought from an authorized distributor, which was assumed to be original.

Boot Device: Only had one SD card, so set the bootloader to USB mode and attempted to boot from a USB 3.0 flash drive.

Bootloader Repair: Installed the bootloader on the SD card, got the green screen, but did not know whether anything else was required.

Various Boot Methods Tried:

- Power + SD card
- Power + USB flash drive
- Power alone

The sole indication of activity (apart from the blinking error code) was when attempting to use the bootloader tool.

Next Steps Recommended by the Community

Boot with only a power supply and HDMI—nothing else plugged in.

If the error continues, the problem may be:

1. A defective or incompatible SD card

2. Defective firmware in the Raspberry Pi

3. An issue introduced by the case or cooler setup

Potential Firmware Solution

- The customer asked if there was a possibility to reset the firmware to factory settings.

- A community member suggested trying to flash the EEPROM recovery image in the Raspberry Pi Imager, ensuring that it was the correct one for the Raspberry Pi 5, not the Pi 4.

- The user searched in the Raspberry Pi Imager's utility section but found only boot configuration tools.

- Another member clarified that these tools reflash the firmware with a default config, essentially resetting it.

Final Attempt & Conclusion

The user concluded they might need to purchase a new SD card and was going to try that next.

Key Takeaway:

If you're having the same boot issues with Raspberry Pi 5, start with a new SD card with Raspberry Pi OS and an adequate power supply. If the problem persists, try reloading the firmware through the EEPROM recovery tool.

TROUBLESHOOTING COMMON ISSUES WITH RASPBERRY PI CONNECT

If you're running into problems with Raspberry Pi Connect, here are some of the most common issues and how to check if they're affecting you:

1. "Unable to locate package rpi-connect" Error

If you're trying to install `rpi-connect` but getting an error saying it can't be found, it's likely because you're not using the correct version of Raspberry Pi OS. Raspberry Pi Connect is only available on Raspberry Pi OS Bookworm.

To check which version you're running, enter this command:

```sh
cat /etc/os-release
```

If your system doesn't show "Debian GNU/Linux 12 (bookworm)" or "Raspbian GNU/Linux 12 (bookworm)", you'll need to update to Raspberry Pi OS Bookworm.

2. Screen Sharing Not Working / WayVNC Won't Start

If Raspberry Pi Connect says screen sharing is "unavailable", it means it can't communicate with the WayVNC service, which is required for this feature to work. To check its status, run:

```sh
systemctl --user status rpi-connect-wayvnc
journalctl --user --follow --unit rpi-connect-wayvnc
```

If WayVNC isn't running or the service can't be found, make sure:

You're using rpi-connect version 1.1.0 or newer (avoid `rpi-connect-lite`, which doesn't support screen sharing).

You're using a Wayland compositor like Wayfire (which is on by default for Raspberry Pi 4 and 5 with OS Bookworm). X11 is not supported.

Your desktop environment supports WayVNC, such as Raspberry Pi Desktop. (KDE isn't compatible because it switches to an unsupported compositor, `kwin`.)

An active desktop session is running under the same user you're signed in with. If necessary, turn on Desktop Autologin in `raspi-config` under System Options.

3. Can't Connect After a Restart or When Closing an SSH Session

Raspberry Pi Connect is a user-level service, so it only works when the user is actively signed in. If you're having trouble reconnecting after a reboot or when your SSH session ends, here's what to do:

For remote shell access without needing an active session, enable user-lingering so Raspberry Pi Connect stays running at all times.

For screen sharing, keep in mind that Raspberry Pi Connect does not create a new desktop session—it only shares an existing one. If you want it to be available right from startup, enable Desktop Autologin in `raspi-config` under System Options.

4. Network and Firewall Problems

Raspberry Pi Connect is designed to work without making network or firewall changes, but if you're on a restricted network and having trouble, check these points:

Make sure you can reach the Raspberry Pi Connect API, which is needed for authentication and connection setup. Try opening this link in your browser:

 https://api.connect.raspberrypi.com/up

Ensure access to the STUN server (`stun.raspberrypi.com`) on UDP port 3478, which helps set up peer-to-peer connections.

Check if you can connect to the TURN servers (`turn1.raspberrypi.com`, `turn2.raspberrypi.com`, `turn3.raspberrypi.com`) on these ports:

- TCP: 3478 or 443
- UDP: 3478, 443, and 49152-65535

If these connections are blocked, you may need to adjust your firewall settings or contact your network administrator.

COMMON HARDWARE AND SOFTWARE ISSUES

Raspberry Pi 5 Not Booting: HDMI and Firmware Issues

I am experiencing critical boot and display issues with my Raspberry Pi 5, and after numerous troubleshooting attempts, I am still not able to get it working. Following is a summary of the problem and the steps I have taken so far:

HDMI Issues

HDMI 0 (the one closest to the power cord): The display flashes on and off, green static and terrible signal.

HDMI 1: Worked once upon first time, but now does not even recognize any signal whatsoever. Port neither one is currently working.

Boot Problems

My Raspberry Pi 5 won't boot from SD cards that boot flawlessly on my Raspberry Pi 4B.

I've done multiple EEPROM firmware updates, SD card re-flashes, and hardware tests, none of which have resolved the issue.

EEPROM Recovery Attempts

Followed the official recovery procedure with `rpi-boot-eeprom-recovery-2024-11-12-2712` from Raspberry Pi's GitHub.

Tried two different SD cards (including an 8GB FAT32-formatted card).

Green LED blinks consistently, but the recovery never completes—even after waiting 15+ minutes.

I also attempted recovery using a USB flash drive, but with the same issue persisting.

Steps I've Taken

Firmware and Recovery Attempts

Updated EEPROM firmware using `rpi-boot-eeprom-recovery-2024-11-12-2712-sd.zip` and ensured all the necessary files (`recovery.bin`, `pieeprom.bin`, etc.) were correctly placed in the root of the SD card.

Tested with multiple SD cards (16GB, 8GB, 256GB), all formatted FAT32 with Master Boot Record (MBR).

Hardware Testing

Tested two different mini-HDMI cables and different monitors—same issue persists.

Tested the same setup (monitors, cables, SD cards, power supply) on a Raspberry Pi 4B, which worked flawlessly.

Confirmed that my 27W USB-C Raspberry Pi power supply is delivering enough power.

Other Recovery Techniques

Attempted to press and hold the reset button during power-up, but no luck.

Next Steps?

I now believe there is a hardware issue with the HDMI ports or the EEPROM. I did not want to assume it's a faulty unit yet, so I was hoping someone has additional troubleshooting I can try.

RASPBERRY PI 5 ISSUE

I'm experiencing an issue with my Raspberry Pi 5, even after performing a fresh installation of the Raspberry Pi OS. The problem keeps appearing in my system logs, and I'm unsure how to resolve it.

System Details:

Kernel Version: 6.6.28+rpt-rpi-2712 #1 SMP PREEMPT Debian 1:6.6.28-1+rpt1 (2024-04-22) aarch64 GNU/Linux

Error Message:

In my `dmesg` log, I repeatedly see this message:

```

[  407.041871] raspberrypi-firmware soc:firmware: Request 0x00030002 returned status 0x00000000

```

It also appears in my system journal:

```

kernel: raspberrypi-firmware soc:firmware: Request 0x00030002 returned status 0x00000000
```

```
```

This is the only error highlighted in red in my logs, and I don't fully understand what it means.

Possible Causes and Troubleshooting

A Raspberry Pi engineer suggested that the issue could be caused by a few factors, including:

- Faulty hardware
- Insufficient power supply
- System instability due to overclocking
- Software-related problems

To help diagnose the problem, they asked if the error appears immediately after booting on a fresh OS installation or only after running certain applications. They also asked if I had any peripherals connected (USB devices, HATs, SSDs, etc.).

I was also advised to share the output of the following command:

```
raspinfo | pastebinit
```

My Setup and Observations

I am using the original power adapter that came with the Raspberry Pi, purchased from an official retailer.

I haven't modified the hardware in any way, nor have I overclocked or undervolted the system.

The error does not appear right away. It only starts showing up in my logs after I connect to the internet following my initial setup.

Steps Taken Before Connecting to the Internet

Before going online, I performed several system-hardening steps based on recommendations from [this security guide](https://madaidans-insecurities.github.io/guides/linux-hardening.html).

Initial Configurations:

1. Used `raspi-config` to apply basic settings.

2. Disabled onboard Wi-Fi and Bluetooth by adding the following lines to `/boot/firmware/config.txt`:

```
dtoverlay=disable-wifi
dtoverlay=disable-bt
```

(Rebooted to apply changes.)

3. Removed passwordless `sudo` privileges from `/etc/sudoers.d/010_pi-nopasswd`.

4. Enabled AppArmor by adding `lsm=apparmor` to `/boot/firmware/cmdline.txt`.

5. Disabled core dumps in `/etc/security/limits.conf` to prevent data leaks:

```
hard core 0
soft core 0
```

6. Added login warning messages to `/etc/issue` and `/etc/issue.net`:

```
@@@@@@@@@@@@@@@@@@@@@@@@@@@@@@@@@@@@@@@@@@@@@@@@@@
    IF YOU ARE NOT ME, STAY AWAY FROM THIS PC!
@@@@@@@@@@@@@@@@@@@@@@@@@@@@@@@@@@@@@@@@@@@@@@@@@@
```

Kernel and Network Hardening

I modified `/etc/sysctl.conf` to apply security-focused kernel and network settings, such as:

Disabling auto-loading of certain kernel modules.

Enforcing stricter network rules to protect against attacks like IP spoofing and man-in-the-middle attacks.

Disabling unnecessary network protocols.

Removing Unnecessary Software

I also removed various packages and services that I deemed unnecessary or potentially vulnerable, including:

- Printer services (`cups`, `pi-printer-support`)
- SSH (`ssh`, `openssh`)
- Compilers (`gcc`, `g++`)
- Camera-related software (`libcamera`, `libdc1394`)
- The `avahi-daemon` service

Final Steps

After applying these changes, I rebooted the system to ensure everything was set correctly.

At this point, the system runs fine until I connect to the internet. That's when the error message starts appearing. I'm not sure if my security settings are interfering with the firmware or if there's another underlying issue.

Has anyone else experienced something similar or found a solution?

PERFORMANCE OPTIMIZATION AND COOLING

Raspberry Pi engineers have fine-tuned the Pi 5's memory settings, making it 10-20% faster at its standard 2.4 GHz speed. Naturally, I had to test overclocking—and with these tweaks, I managed to push the Pi 5 to 3.2 GHz, achieving a 32% speed boost!

These improvements could soon be included in a firmware update for both Raspberry Pi 5 and Pi 4 users.

What's Changing and Why It Matters

A while ago, I set a Geekbench 6 world record on the Pi 5, but someone later broke my score using special cooling and NUMA emulation tricks. Now, Raspberry Pi's engineers have taken things further by fine-tuning SDRAM (memory) timings to make the Pi run even faster.

The Pi was previously running its memory refresh settings at the default manufacturer rate, but engineers found out that Micron's 8GB SDRAM chips can actually handle faster 4GB refresh rates. This allows the Pi to refresh memory less frequently, reducing overhead and improving speed—especially for multi-core tasks, but also for single-core performance.

While both Pi 4 and Pi 5 benefit from these tweaks, the Pi 5 sees the biggest improvements thanks to faster memory, wider data paths, and better SDRAM access.

How to Enable the Faster Memory Settings

These improvements might soon be included by default, but if you want to try them now, follow these steps:

1. Update your Pi's firmware by running:

```sh
sudo rpi-update
```

(Press Y to confirm.)

2. Edit the bootloader configuration:

```sh
sudo rpi-eeprom-config -e
```

3. Add the following line:

For Pi 5:

```
SDRAM_BANKLOW=1
```

For Pi 4:

```
SDRAM_BANKLOW=3
```

4. Save the changes and reboot your Raspberry Pi.

NUMA Emulation for Even More Speed

Raspberry Pi OS now includes NUMA emulation, which helps manage memory even more efficiently.

To enable NUMA:

1. Update your system with:

```sh
sudo apt full-upgrade
```

2. Check if NUMA is working by running:

```sh
dmesg | grep NUMA
```

If you see something like this:

```
mempolicy: NUMA default policy overridden to 'interleave:0-7'
```

it means NUMA is active!

If you need to tweak settings, you can edit `/boot/firmware/cmdline.txt` and add:

```
numa=fake=[n]
```

But for most users, the default settings should work just fine.

Overclocking: Pushing the Pi 5 Even Further

I wanted to see just how much faster the Pi 5 could go, so I overclocked it using my custom overclocking guide.

Here's what I added to `/boot/firmware/config.txt`:

```
over_voltage_delta=72000
arm_freq=3200
gpu_freq=1000
```

After rebooting, I:

Maxed out my cooling fan to prevent overheating.

Used my pi-overvolt tool to increase voltage.

Set the CPU to performance mode with:

```sh
echo performance | sudo tee /sys/devices/system/cpu/cpu/cpufreq/scaling_governor
```

How Much Faster Did It Get?

With just the memory tweaks, I saw an 8% increase in single-core speed and an 18% boost in multi-core speed.

But at 3.2 GHz, my Geekbench scores jumped by 32% (single-core) and 31% (multi-core), setting another world record!

Benchmark	Default Pi 5	With SDRAM + NUMA	With 3.2 GHz Overclock
Single-Core	833	899 (+8%)	1153 (+32%)
Multi-Core	1805	2169 (+32%)	2468 (+31%)

I ran these tests using only an Argon THRML 30-AC Active Cooler, with the fan running at 100% to keep temperatures in check.

Overclocking Limits: How Far Can the Pi 5 Go?

After testing 20 different Raspberry Pi 5 boards, I found:

- Most can easily handle 2.6 or 2.8 GHz.

- About half can reach 3.0 GHz.

- Very few can go beyond 3.1 GHz.

- Extreme overclocking (3.4 GHz+) is rare and highly unstable, even with advanced cooling.

With the new SDRAM tweaks, memory timing becomes even more sensitive, so pushing the Pi past 3.2 GHz is tricky.

Final Thoughts

These optimizations might soon become standard, as some users have already noticed higher Geekbench scores on Pi 500 models since September.

For a while, slow memory speeds were a weak spot for the Pi 5, especially compared to RK3588 boards. But these new tweaks give the Pi 5 a major speed boost—over a year after its release!

EXPANDING RASPBERRY PI'S CAPABILITIES

Pineboards is leading the way in expanding the capabilities of the Raspberry Pi 5, introducing a series of HATs and PCIe-based accessories that provide faster storage, better networking, and enhanced connectivity. These add-ons make the Pi 5 even more versatile, allowing it to be used in a variety of demanding applications.

Innovative New Accessories from Embedded World 2024

NVMe Storage Boards – Pineboards introduced two versions of NVMe storage expansions:

- Top-mounting version for easy access.
- Bottom-mounting version for a cleaner, more compact installation.

2.5 Gigabit Ethernet Card – The first-ever 2.5GbE expansion for Raspberry Pi 5, with much quicker networking speeds—perfect for data-heavy use cases.

PCIe Switch Boards – These boards enable users to connect multiple devices simultaneously, such as:

- Dual NVMe drives for increased storage.
- NVMe drive + AI accelerator (like the Coral TPU) for high-performance image processing and AI workloads.

Why These Upgrades Matter

☑ Enterprise-Level Performance – Brings high-speed storage and networking to the Raspberry Pi 5.

☑ AI and Data Processing – Supports AI-powered applications, real-time data processing, and industrial automation.

☑ Maximizing PCIe Potential – Creates new possibilities for developers, making the Pi 5 more powerful than ever.

Pineboards continues to push the Raspberry Pi 5 to new levels, offering users greater possibilities to customize, optimize, and enhance their projects.

Expanding Raspberry Pi 5 with Pineboards' Latest Upgrades

At Embedded World 2024, Pineboards showcased new expansion accessories designed to enhance the Raspberry Pi 5's capabilities. These demonstrations highlighted how the add-ons improve speed, connectivity, and overall functionality, making the Pi 5 even more powerful for various applications.

Faster and More Efficient Storage

Pineboards introduced two NVMe storage board options—one with a top-mounted design for easy access and another with a bottom-mounted setup for a more compact build.

These upgrades dramatically increase storage speed, making the Raspberry Pi 5 more suitable for demanding computing tasks.

High-Speed Networking with 2.5GbE Ethernet

The new 2.5 Gigabit Ethernet expansion is the fastest available networking solution for the Raspberry Pi 5.

It's ideal for network storage (NAS), IoT applications, and industrial monitoring systems that require fast and reliable data transfer.

More Connectivity with PCIe Expansion

The PCIe switch board allows users to connect multiple devices to the Raspberry Pi 5's single PCIe lane.

Demonstrations included running two NVMe drives at once and integrating an AI accelerator for machine learning applications.

Why These Add-Ons Matter

- These upgrades make the Raspberry Pi 5 much more versatile, whether for personal projects or professional applications.

- They enable advanced features like AI development, edge computing, and high-speed data processing, pushing the Raspberry Pi 5 beyond its standard capabilities.

Looking Ahead: The Future of Raspberry Pi 5 Expansion

With the Raspberry Pi 5 gaining popularity, expansion solutions like Pineboards' add-ons are becoming essential for users who want to get the most out of their device. These enhancements not only boost performance but also introduce features usually found in enterprise-level hardware. As Pineboards continues to develop new solutions, the Raspberry Pi 5's potential keeps growing, opening up exciting possibilities for customization and high-performance computing.

INDEX